About the authors

Nana K. Poku is the John Ferguson Professor of African
Studies at the University of Bradford. He joined the
university's Peace Studies Department in 2006 from the
United Nations, where he held the posts of senior policy
adviser to the executive secretary of the Economic Commission for Africa (ECA) and director of research for the
Commission on HIV/AIDS and Governance in Africa
(UN-CHGA). He currently serves as a special adviser to
the government of Ghana on PRSP and health issues and
has led fourteen appraisal missions in eleven countries
in Africa. He has also been an adviser to the European
Union, the World Bank, the Organisation for Economic
Co-operation and Development, the World Health
Organization and the United Nations Development Programme, among other international agencies.

Anna Mdee is deputy director of the John and Elnora
Ferguson Centre for African Studies (JEFCAS) and also
Associate Dean (Teaching & Learning) in the School
of Social and International Studies at the University of
Bradford. Her research has focused on aid policy, civil
society and community-driven development in East and
southern Africa. She is currently working on developing
strategic partnerships with African universities to build
long-term initiatives for strengthening development
research and teaching.

POLITICS IN AFRICA
a new introduction

Nana K. Poku and Anna Mdee

Zed Books
LONDON · NEW YORK

Politics in Africa: a new introduction was first published in 2011 by
Zed Books Ltd, 7 Cynthia Street, London N1 9JF, UK and Room 400,
175 Fifth Avenue, New York, NY 10010, USA

www.zedbooks.co.uk

FSC
www.fsc.org
MIX
Paper from
responsible sources
FSC® C013604

Set in Monotype Sabon and Gill Sans Heavy by
Ewan Smith, London
Index: <ed.emery@thefreeuniversity.net>
Cover designed by Stuart Tolley
Printed and bound in Great Britain by CPI Antony
Rowe, Chippenham and Eastbourne

Distributed in the USA exclusively by Palgrave Macmillan, a division of
St Martin's Press, LLC, 175 Fifth Avenue, New York, NY 10010, USA

A catalogue record for this book is available from the British Library
Library of Congress Cataloging in Publication Data available

ISBN 978 1 84277 981 1 hb
ISBN 978 1 84277 982 8 pb

Contents

Figures and tables

Abbreviations

AIDS	Acquired Immunodeficiency Syndrome
AISPs	Agricultural Input Subsidies Programmes
ANC	African National Congress
AU	African Union
CAADP	Comprehensive Africa Agriculture Development Programme
CEDAW	(UN) Convention on the Elimination of All Forms of Discrimination against Women
FAO	Food and Agriculture Organization of the United Nations
GAD	Gender and Development
GDP	gross domestic product
GFATM	Global Fund to Fight AIDS, Tuberculosis and Malaria
GM	genetically modified
GNP	gross national product
HIPC	Heavily Indebted Poor Countries
HIV	Human Immunodeficiency Virus
IFPRI	International Food Policy Research Institute
IMF	International Monetary Fund
MDGs	Millennium Development Goals
NEPAD	New Partnership for Africa's Development
NGO	non-governmental organization
OECD	Organisation for Economic Co-operation and Development
PEPFAR	President's Emergency Plan for AIDS Relief (United States)
SAP	structural adjustment programme
SSA	sub-Saharan Africa
STI	sexually transmitted infection
UN	United Nations
UNCTAD	United Nations Conference on Trade and Development
WB	World Bank
WID	Women in Development

Acknowledgements

Putting together this book has not been an easy process and we must relay our thanks to those who have supported us in bringing it to completion. Much appreciation is due to Ken Barlow of Zed Books for patiently cajoling us to make progress despite endless missed deadlines, to Jacqueline Therkelsen for tirelessly tidying up our referencing and textual inconsistencies, and also to Lisa Thorley and Isaac Kankam-Boadu for the detailed background research which underpins Chapter 3.

This book is dedicated to Professor Tony Barnett for his contribution to the study of African societies, politics and culture.

Introduction

Self-determination, prosperity and progress – this was the dream of African independence. For a people who had for many centuries been little more than objects of external rivalries, independence was an opportunity to prove, in the words of Habib Bourguiba, Tunisia's head of government in 1961, that 'the African was capable of running his own affairs; fighting his own battles and developing his own people' (Davidson 1964). Kwame Nkrumah, the founding father of Ghana, came to symbolize this new-found confidence. Upon hearing in 1957 that Félix Houphouët-Boigny of Côte d'Ivoire favoured greater fraternity with France rather than full independence, Nkrumah's advice to him was unambiguous: 'seek ye first the political kingdom and all shall be added unto you' (Busia 1967). The advice, though heady, must be seen in the context of the time; the whole colonial system functioned on the conviction that the Europeans were superior, that their subjects – who by definition were inferior – neither understood nor wanted self-government. For leaders of the African independence movements, therefore, independence was an opportunity to demonstrate not only their qualities as human beings, but also their competence as state managers. Again Nkrumah offers insight: 'with self government, we'll transform Africa into a paradise in ten years' (Nkrumah 1957).

The wheels of fate did not permit Nkrumah a full decade of power. By the time of his political demise in 1966, Ghana was far from being a paradise, locked, as it was, into a pattern of corruption, stagnation and conflict, which persists to the present. Today, it is hard to escape the painful reality that 'all else' has not followed. The early optimism has long faded, the enormous challenge of self-government, nation-building and development assuming ever more challenging realities in a fundamentally transformed continental and global landscape. In the interim, Claude Ake offers the following indictment of post-colonial rule: 'indigenous leaders are responsible for a perverse alienation, the delinking of leaders from followers, a weak sense of national identity and the perception of the government as a hostile force' (Ake 1996). The resulting social decay presents a dramatic picture of insecurity for ordinary people in circumstances where states have proved either unable to provide their protection or in some cases were the principal sources of violence.

A common theme runs through virtually all the predictions made of the continent. The vast landmass appears to be cited in order to stress its transience or decrepitude, as if some curse of dubious scientific basis had been laid on political analysis of the whole continent. Ignored by theoreticians and discredited by militant attackers of imperialism whose dialectical reasoning proved Africa's impotence in global politics, the continent now appears to exist only as a reminder of the failures of indigenous rule. In retrospect, even the colonial regimes have gained a certain measure of respect: Johnson U. J. Asiegbu, for example, found it possible to contrast the 'patriotism and probity, [...] self-discipline' and other remarkable ideals of public responsibility of the colonial period with the 'bad and dishonest examples, [...] the criminal wastage, the fraudulent and selfish mismanagement of the continent's resources practised by the new "predatory elites" in post-colonial Africa' (Asiegbu 1984).

There is no denying the facts to which these conclusions speak: to the extent that international calculations of national poverty indices can be trusted, Africans are not yet the poorest people in the world. Only 23 per cent of the continent's population of 850 million were classified by the World Bank as poor in 2010; this proportion is nowhere close to the 40 per cent poverty-afflicted population among Asia's 2.2 billion people (World Bank 2010). Yet Africa's consistently declining rates of economic productivity and surging population growth portend deepening impoverishment, compared with South Asia, where an increase in per capita income is already evident. Moreover, for most people, the heart-rending pictures of starving children in Ethiopia or young people suffering from the debilitating and dehumanizing effects of the HI virus (HIV), the atrocities of Darfur or Rwanda, the absurd posturing of Robert Mugabe or Omar Hassan Ahmad al-Bashir make up the primary picture of the continent.

In reality, there is more to modern Africa than a vast list of failures. Undoubtedly, self-rule as perverted by indigenous African elites is an important factor in accounting for the continent's current malaise, but is it any more so than the legacies of colonialism or Africa's place in the global economy? Through much of the continent, ordinary people and officials are grappling with a host of issues and crises within the financial and technical limitations that lie so heavily upon them. Political parties and civil society organizations operate in many countries, by no means always under the oppressive gaze of dictatorial or autocratic regimes, as is sometimes commonly supposed outside the continent. Local communities discuss seriously the problems of education, health and livelihoods, while resolving conflicts and pushing for compromises as the need arises. In short, a real learning curve can be discerned. Governments have finally started to sift sense out of nonsense. They have, in the words of former Zambian president Kenneth Kaunda, 'begun to take responsibility for their misguided actions while recognising that their countries are bleeding from self-inflected wounds' (Poku 2013).

The chapters that make up this book are better viewed as a series of interpretative essays that draw on a variety of sources with the explicit aim of placing, within an overall perspective, a broad range of modern political developments on the African continent. Yet the book is neither intended as a chronology of history nor a chronological study of contemporary events; both tasks are too vast and complex for any single volume. Besides, there are many books currently available; this means that the specialist and even the non-specialist will be aware of the many omissions in these pages. We are aware of them ourselves. Yet those omissions may be forgiven for the sake of clarity and readability within a relatively short volume, which is designed to offer a framework for understanding contemporary events and issues. Accordingly, what follows here is a rather modest attempt to equip readers with a sound understanding of continental themes which will enable them to analyse and make sense of their complexities, and objectively contribute to some of the major debates that preoccupy scholars of the continent.

A central feature of our analysis, therefore, is an exploration of the interplay between *contingency* (the unintended effects of colonial legacies); *choice* (the corrosive effects of post-colonial policies, leadership and governance); and the *structural influences* on development (Africa in the global economic system). It may be charged that such an argument risks encouraging the tendency to find excuses for failure on the African continent in the heritage of colonialism or the machinations of outside forces, and that it is time we stopped blaming everything on the colonial past. To this charge our response comes in the form of a responsibility to focus on the failings of Africa's political elites; to analyse which of the many failings are intrinsic to the condition in which colonialism left the continent and which, given clearer purpose and properly pursued, might have been surmounted. In the process we shall examine the state structures built up during the colonial period and taken over at the time of independence and how, in the phase of decolonization and beyond, African elites have sought to utilize their power.

The size and variety of the African continent, which makes any generalization difficult, is perhaps too obvious a point to labour. However, it is the necessary starting point. No matter how they are viewed, the people of Africa are arranged into patterns of great diversity. The shortest-statured people in the world (Pygmoids) live in close proximity to the tallest (Tutsi). Skin tones vary widely across the continent. Subsistence modes cover a spectrum from Palaeolithic-like hunting and gathering to nomadic pastoralism, to shifting cultivation, to paddy-rice cultivation, to livestock ranching, to dairy farming, and to all the occupations associated with urban industrial society. Islam, in its several traditions, and all conceivable forms of Christianity are intermixed with traditional forms of worship, and in some cases the contact has produced 'new' forms of syncretic religions. This recitation could be continued almost indefinitely and represents only a snapshot of the richness of the African experience.

For some students in the West, this awareness of Africa's utterly unfamiliar environment can easily produce a despairing conviction that it is impossible to understand people and societies so different. Such a lament is understandable, but it is necessarily defeatist. It also negates the central principle of social sciences; by observation, careful probing and empathy, good scholars can detach themselves from the confines of their own history and enter into the perceptions and prejudices of those they study. It is not easy and no doubt mistakes will be made. Yet to deny the possibility is to condemn us to wallowing in the backwaters of our own narrow worlds; this applies equally to some African scholars who sometimes despair about oversimplification and exaggerated portrayal of their continent by outsiders.

Structure of the book

In reading this book, our hope is that a general reader will gain sufficient understanding of the complex political history of the continent to enable them to fit the confusing array of men and events into a framework of general patterns. For the serious student of Africa, we hope to use the empirical analysis of recent African political history to throw some light on general principles.

The book is divided into five chapters. The first two provide a foundational analysis relating to the intellectual political economy and history of the African continent. They consider the formation of the African state and its evolution since pre-colonial times to the present day. In doing so, we seek to contextualize our analysis of contemporary political challenges in Africa in Chapters 3, 4 and 5. In a short volume such as this, space is never sufficient to satisfy every point of analysis or pertinent and important issue. Our perspective always attempts to complexify rather than simplify, to present a holistic yet digestible analysis and to raise more questions than answers.

ONE

Colonialism, racism and African resistance

It is surprising for many students that most of the African continent was under European control for less than a seventy-year period and that the Congress of Berlin which initiated this took place just over 120 years ago. Yet in this relatively short period, massive changes took place on the continent that not only established the immediate context of African politics, but also continue to constrain and shape its future to this day. The purpose of this chapter is not to detail Africa's colonial history or indeed its many legacies, but to outline some of the debates around each, which have relevance for our understanding of Africa today. We need to consider the explanations of the 'scramble' and of the colonization that followed the Congress of Berlin in 1884 within the context of ideology, commerce, resistance and liberation. In so doing, the chapter will highlight two things: impact and continuity. It draws obvious attention to the impact of the years of imperial rule, but the chapter also assumes an element of continuity, a degree of initiative and autonomy, on the part of those subject to foreign rule. Importantly, both forces – impact and continuity – established the environment for politics of the new state at the time of independence – the subject of the next chapter.

The scramble for Africa

Colonialism is a general term signifying domination and hegemony, classically in the form of political rule and economic control on the part of a European state over territories and peoples outside Europe. The earliest forms of colonialism in this sense (not all empires were colonial empires) were exhibited in the New World by Spain and Portugal, although classical colonialism flowered later only in conjunction with the rise of global capitalism, manifested in the rule by European states over various polities in Asia and Africa. Imperialism as a term is sometimes seen as interchangeable with colonialism, even as it has often been used to focus on the economic, and specifically capitalist, character of colonial rule. Colonialism itself has sometimes been reserved for cases of settler colonialism, where segments of the dominant population not only rule over, but settle in, colonial territories. However, most scholars agree that colonialism was in fact a form of rule that was most often not accompanied by European settlement, and that the term 'colonialism' entails sustained control over a local population by states that were interested in neither settlement nor assimilation.

Allied to both colonialism and imperialism was the notion of enlightenment; more precisely, discovery and reason. Reason gave discovery a justification and a new meaning, but it also took its expanding global laboratory for granted. Science flourished in the eighteenth century not merely because of the intense curiosity of individuals working in Europe, but because colonial expansion both necessitated and facilitated the active exercise of the scientific imagi-nation. It was through discovery – the seeking, surveying, mapping, naming and ultimately possessing – of new regions that science itself could open new territories of conquest, among them cartography, geography, botany, philology and anthropology. As the world was literally shaped for Europe through cartography – which, writ large, encompassed the narration of ship logs and route maps, the drawing of boundaries, the extermination of 'natives', the settling of peoples, the appropriation of property, the assessment of revenue, the raising of flags, and the writing of new histories – it was also parcelled into clusters of colonized territories to be controlled by increasingly power-ful European nations, the Dutch, French and British in particular.

With the benefit of hindsight it is possible to see how European intellectuals became colonialism's greatest champions. Hegel (1956), for example, in his introduction to *The Philosophy of History*, offers the following: 'The Negro represents natural man in all his wild and untamed nature. If you want to treat and understand him right, you must abstract all elements of respect and morality and sensitivity – there is nothing remotely humanised in the Negro's character [...] nothing confirms this judgement more than the reports of missionaries.'

In other words, if Europeans were enslaving and treating Africans as they did, Africans had to be thought of as animals or at best subhuman; the God-fearing Caucasian was incapable of treating 'brothers in Christ' in such inhuman ways (Eze 1997). Arguably, it was this inversion of reason and morality which set the scene for the advent of nineteenth- and twentieth-century scientific racism with surprising effect on the European intellectual class. Liberals like Hobson cast their vote against empire, while Marx, ambiguously, regarded imperialism as morally repugnant, but historically progressive. Similarly, Mill had no difficulties in accepting that the civilized had special rights over, but also obligations towards, barbarians and savages, while also advocating a world order based on the right of national self-determination.

Africans resisted colonialism. They resisted it by force and they resisted it culturally and intellectually. There were many examples of this type of resistance. They ranged from the rising by the Mahdists in the Sudan (General Gordon and all that, 1884) through religious oppositional cults such as Mumboism in Kenya (1913–58) to refusal to pay hut and head tax in many places, refusal to work on plantations and to adopt agricultural and other types of innovation, and, perhaps of greatest lasting importance, the development of 'voluntary associations' in most parts of Africa, urban organizations which quickly took on a quasi or explicitly political complexion. However, by the mid-nineteenth century, African-ness and 'the negro' were well established as low points in the consciousness of Europe. W. E. B. Du Bois (1964: 39) was later to conclude that 'never in modern times has [so] large a section of [any society] so used its combined intellectual energies to the degradation of [black humanity]'.

As Edward Said suggests in his book *Orientalism* (1979), if 'the Orient' was created as an object to be studied as exotic and 'other', and thus alienated from the mainstream of the world (meaning European) history, then this is also true of Africa. What we see is cultural dehumanization and alienation in the European perception of Africa. It is this dehumanization which explains why the cultural battle was so important and shows us how brave were people who raised dissenting voices to the imperial orthodoxies (as were those European intellectuals who allied themselves with this view). In his important survey of 'African and Third World theories of imperialism', Thomas Hodgkin suggests the following periodization of such resistance: the late nineteenth century (writers such as Blyden) in the period of imperial expansion; 1900–45, the period of partially effective colonial domination, notably the francophone African writers associated with the cultural/political movement known as *négritude*, including Lamine (Leopold) Senghor, Emile Faure, Garan Kouyaté and Aimé Césaire; and the post-1945 phase, concerned with the more active political leaders, Kwame Nkrumah (*Towards Colonial Freedom*, emphasizing pan-African ideals), Julius Nyerere (*Ujamaa: Essays on Socialism*, emphasizing African socialism) and Frantz Fanon (*The Wretched of the Earth*), who concerns himself with the impact of colonialism on the personalities of the colonized and the colonizers (Owen and Sutcliffe 1972). Most of this thought in the twentieth century was to a greater or lesser degree influenced by Marxism, which is unsurprising as this was the main oppositional ideology, with its own power bloc.

An important intellectual/cultural/political strand, most of all among francophone Africans, is identified with the name of Senghor. Senghor (b. 1906), a colonized French soldier, member of the French National Assembly, poet, member of the Académie Française, later president of Senegal, was representative of much in the whole culture of *négritude*. He was very intellectual, scholarly, literary and French. The titles of his essays indicate the seriousness of his thought and also the debt it owes to French culture: 'African metaphysic', 'The relevance of Marx to Africa', 'No political liberation without cultural liberation'. However, the point about *négritude* is that it arose in response to French assimilationist policies (turning Africans into Frenchmen) and said there is much in African culture which is important and valuable. Arguably it was a step in a dialectical movement, which sought to bring white and black together in a classless society.

As such, the notion that *négritude* was racist is profoundly inaccurate. In truth, the movement was not a negation of others; rather it was an affirmation of Africa's contribution to the universal culture. As Senghor says, 'Africa's misfortune has been that our secret enemies, in defending their values, have made us despise our own.' Whereas in fact: 'Négritude is a part of Africanity. It is made of human warmth. It is democracy quickened by the sense of communion and brotherhood between men. More deeply, in works of art, which are a people's most authentic expression of themselves, it is sense of image and rhythm, sense of symbol and beauty' (Senghor 1950).

It was ultimately this curious identity of interest between the diasporic character of the disciples of *négritude* and the fact that French was the only medium available to them to communicate which created the impression of racism. By adopting the French language, these writers found themselves in the paradoxical situation of espousing the very culture that they appeared to be bent on rejecting. As Sartre points out, 'they speak in order to destroy the language in which the oppressor is present: their main project is to "de-gallicize" its signifiers' (Sartre 1979).

A more recent development from this tradition in an unexpected form appears in the work of Bernal. In his book *Black Athena* (1991), Bernal suggests that before the late eighteenth century in Europe, it was well known that classical Greece was deeply rooted culturally and linguistically to the south and the east, in Ancient Egypt (Africa) and in Palestine (Phoenicians, Jews), rather than in some northern invasion. The response to this knowledge in the nineteenth century and after was to suppress it because it did not fit in with European racial prejudices. Bernal does not make this argument lightly; he supports it with a wealth of scholarship. The impact of the book among black American intellectuals has been enormous. Bernal has become a cause célèbre. In some American departments of black studies, people are now taught that all knowledge comes from Africa and that all European knowledge is to be dismissed as racist (although some of it certainly is). This, in our view, is as racist a response as any other and a response that threatens to throw out the rational baby with the white racist bathwater.

The facts are that Bernal's book redresses the balance. Used wrongly, it leads to irrationalism. Now this is perhaps an obscure example, but the unbalancing effect of recognizing racism in scholarship and then dismissing all scholarship is more profound in another area, the research on AIDS. In their book *AIDS, Africa and Racism* (1989), R. and R. Chirimuuta argue that most of the research on AIDS in Africa has tended to blame Africa and Africans for the disease, and that this is a racist conspiracy, when in fact AIDS may well be the result of escapes from germ warfare laboratories – see Chapter 5. There seems little evidence for this latter point. What does seem to be the case is that HIV may have originated in Africa, that around 38 million people are infected, and that the Western press has often made, and continues to make, the link between sexuality, race and disease. However, all this should not lead us to dismiss the results of research that produces information of use in fighting an epidemic disease. The point is that just because the balance has gone one way (suppressing African history and culture, racism) we should always be careful not to let the balance swing the other way in order to assuage our liberal consciences. We must remain critical of the way that all knowledge is constructed.

However, the more pointedly political expressions of African thought in the period before independence and in the 1960s and 1970s emphasized the socialistic and pan-African nature of African thought and tradition. The two most influential writers here are probably Kwame Nkrumah and Julius Nyerere, although Senghor's *On African Socialism* was also important. The former, educated in Britain, leader of the Ghanaian independence movement and first president of Ghana, emphasized the need for African unity and a common position vis-à-vis the imperialists; Nyerere (1968) argued that African culture had always been socialist, thus:

> In our traditional African society we were individuals within a community. We took care of the community and the community took care of us. We neither needed nor wished to exploit our fellow men and in rejecting the capitalist attitudes of mind which colonialism brought into Africa, we must reject also the capitalist methods which go with it. To us in Africa land was always recognised as belonging to the community [...] the foundation and the objective of African socialism is the extended family.

These important philosophical positions, pan-Africanism and socialism, were the organizing principles of the independence struggles and the early years after independence. In Tanzania, the idea received its fullest expression in the official policy of *ujamaa*, and it is here that we learn a depressing lesson. *Ujamaa* turned into statist direction of the peasantry; in Ghana, the Convention People's Party became a site of corruption and oppression. Pan-Africanism received much formal support, but the institutions were not developed. Indeed, the Organization of African Unity (OAU) and its successor the African Union (AU) have remained ineffective and conservative, while African states have had diverse interests and have been the plaything of individual rulers and the victims of dabbling by foreign powers. With the changes in South Africa, even that unifying issue has become a less certain reference point.

The colonial impress

By the midpoint of the nineteenth century, the European political elite had accepted the civilizing logic of imperialism as propagated by the intellectual class. Empires were, therefore, justified on the basis of good government and the transmission, through education, of civilizing values. As a result, Africa would exist in the European psyche as the barbaric Other, and the point is not whether it had foundation in either logic or reason; it simply offered the legitimacy for the politics of dominance to be pursued against people of difference. At no point was this more evident than in the lead up to the Congress of Berlin of 1884. In the decade leading up to the conference, the chief instigator, King Leopold II of Belgium, summoned a conference in Brussels to which he invited representatives from Europe and America to launch what came to be known as the International African Association. There, in 1876, King Leopold II spoke as a humanitarian, and as one interested in geographic exploration for the sake of science: 'To open to civilization the only part of the globe where it has not yet penetrated, to pierce the darkness shrouding entire populations, that is, if I may venture to say, a crusade worthy of this century of progress.'

However, from beneath King Leopold II's affable altruism there peeped the true intent of European interest in Africa:

> Among those who have most closely studied Africa, a good many have been led to think that there is advantage to the common object they pursued if they could be brought together for the purpose of conference with the object of regulating the march, combining the effort, deriving some profit from all circumstances, and from all resources, and finally, in order to avoid doing the same work twice over. (Legum 1961)

Leopold's persuasive approach dovetailed with that of Prince Otto von Bismarck, the then Chancellor of Germany, intent on preventing any of the large European competitors from gaining advantage in Africa. Under King Leopold of Belgium's pretext of settling the narrow issue of Congo, the Congress of Berlin became the Magna

Carta of the colonial powers in Africa. Because the Congress made effective control of territory the test of ownership, the continent was rapidly occupied and divided. As a result, any European power which, by treaty or conquest, picked out a choice bit of Africa would be recognized as its lawful ruler, provided no other power had already laid claim to it. 'We have been giving mountains and rivers and lakes to each other,' British prime minister Lord Salisbury admitted after the Congress, 'unhindered by the small impediment that we never knew exactly where they were' (cited in Midwinter 2006). They were unhindered as well by the fact that all these lands belonged to others. Over the next fifteen or so years, the European powers consolidated their coastal enclaves and expanded them into the interior. Basically, this involved pushing the borders along the coast until they collided with another European power's borders and then drawing points of contact inland.

Within their colonial boundaries, the colonizers constructed African economies to serve European rather than African interests and integrated African markets into the global division of labour. As large-scale plantations developed and expanded on the continent in order to service European demands, there was also an influx of a significant number of European settlers. These settlers were concentrated heavily in the eastern and southern parts of the continent, as well as in Algeria. Although their numbers were relatively small, paradoxically this was a major source of strength. It provided a very effective way of preserving the assumption of white superiority on which the whole edifice of colonial administration depended. The patents for the administrative grids fashioned in London or Paris, in Brussels or Lisbon, varied in style and design, but colonialism in its different variations (see Table 1.1) was either direct or indirect rule with the norm being a mix of the two.

Direct rule usually involved the breakdown of traditional structures of power and authority, which were replaced with rule by white European administrations whose officers were sent out from the metropole. Direct rule did not spread widely to the countryside except if there existed valuable mineral resources, such as in the Copperbelts of Zambia and Katanga, or concentrations of white European settler-farmers, such as in the highlands of Kenya, Natal, the central highlands of Namibia and southern Rhodesia. However,

TABLE 1.1 Variations in colonial systems

Colonial power	Context	Theory	Practice
French colonialism	Characterized by an emphasis on uniformity of administration (cf. British colonial administration); policy of identity and of paternalism: i) In the early period of French colonialism, the key idea was that of identity: roots in revolutionary tradition of France, 'all men, without distinction of colour, domiciled in French colonies are French citizens, and enjoy all the rights assured by the Constitution' (Decree of 1792 abolishing African slavery). Thus: rights to elect deputies to the National Assembly in Paris; degree of local self-government; public, free, secular education in French language. This policy came to an end in the 19th century and was replaced by: ii) paternalism: conservative and autocratic; weakening of French revolutionary zeal, replacement by ideology of empire and extension of French rule in vast areas of West and Equatorial Africa (as well as the north). 'Citizens' became 'subjects', forced labour, administrative direction, end of participation.	Universal, no racial discrimination; French citizens have equal rights; popular participation at all levels; the French colonies were part of the Republic; meritocracy of education – the notion of assimilation.	*Petit blanc* racialism; dual college in French Africa except in Senegal, Mauritania, Togo, massive weighting to the metropolitan votes; there were African representatives, but they did not have responsible participation in administration; little progress in African education. All of this supported by vast disparities in income and opportunity within a colonial extractive economy.

British colonialism	In contrast to the French approach, characterized by piecemeal pragmatism: the British approach colonial rule with paternalism through the policy of 'indirect rule'. This policy was replaced after WWII by the policy of transition (slow) to the Westminster model; limited participation supported the small educated elite against the 'traditional' authorities. In East Africa a 'colon'-class notion of representation on lines of 'estates', which happened to be racial in derivation – white, Indian, African. The contradictions can be summed up as the differences between theory and practice.	Liberal conception of devolution of powers; legislative councils, parliaments; indirect rule based on relations of sympathy between British administrators and African 'chiefs'; education for leadership in elite schools; 'basic freedoms' as in Britain.	In East Africa and Central African Federation concessions to 'colons', Africans cut out of political process; in West Africa indirect rule through 'chiefs'; weakening of traditional authority, rise of educated elite who were then rejected by the British administration and subjected to restrictions on political activity.
Belgian colonialism (Congo mainly, but also Rwanda and Burundi after 1918)	Congo Free State 1885 excluded from the liberal currents of European thought, idea of 'dominer pour servir' (the title of a book by Pierre Ryckmans). Burgher mentality, 'civilization' = martial success + thrift + self-help + domestic decency. Separate juridical status for Europeans and Africans; mission paternalism education + political power of the large companies. Idea that the Belgians were the 'philosopher kings' and the Africans were the producers. Contradictions can be summed up as the differences between theory and practice.	Belgian emphasis on Calvinist values, Africans could (and did) become 'middle class' – evolué; notion of non-racial Communauté BelgoCongolaise, harmony; alliance of Church and state, both open to Africans; centralization of politics from Brussels, Belgian political parties; insulation of Congo from outside experiment.	No political outlets for the new classes, no trade unions and no civil liberties; racist separatism resented by the 'evolués'; development of millenarian sects to combat Church dominance – Kimbangism; elite demand for more higher education; colon influence, centrifugalism; Congo very open to outside influence.

TABLE 1.1 Variations in colonial systems (continued)

Colonial power	Context	Theory	Practice
Portuguese colonialism	The key feature which distinguishes Portuguese colonialism from the others is that the metropolitan country was itself impoverished, hardly industrialized and in some respects an economic colony itself. In contrast to the ideology of 'free trade' which informed the other colonial systems, in the Portuguese colonies there was (in the main – trade with the Transvaal from Mozambique was the exception) classic mercantilist protection.	The aim was to integrate Africans into Portuguese society, making them into Catholics, Portuguese in culture and part of the money economy. This process was described as 'civilizing'. Africans could apply to the local administration for a certificate to classify them as *civilisado*. This would enable them to enjoy all the rights and obligations of a white Portuguese. Those who were not *civilisados* were *indigenas* and were subject to 'native' law and the rule of chiefs.	In practice, few Africans became *civilisados*. Most remained subject to customary law, paid native tax, were subject to labour obligations. This maintained the structure of African society, provided income for the colonial exchequer and provided a steady stream of cheap labour for government works and for the concessions companies.

it was in urban areas, particularly the colonial capital cities, such as Dakar, Lusaka and Nairobi, that direct rule was mostly exercised.

Indirect rule was most often found in the rural areas that Europeans did not consider suitable for farming and settlement, where no substantial resources, such as minerals, were located, and where the colonial administrative machine found it hardest to permeate owing to the paucity of resources. It was also where there were traditional or customary rulers and authorities who could be authorized and relied upon to maintain order and allegiance to the metropole in return for leaving these indigenous and localized structures of power undisturbed. As Mamdani (1996) makes clear in his *Citizen and Subject*, in non-settler colonies colonialism reinforced and promoted a form of 'customary' power – that is, traditional authority – although this was always subordinated to colonial state rule in order to effect 'indirect rule'. Indirect rule had definite advantages for a colonial regime: it was cheaper to administer and had the effect of boxing African people into discrete ethnic or 'tribal' units maintained by African leaders whose interests were also served by emphasizing and maintaining tribal mentalities among their peoples. Ranger (1996) describes ethnicity as a great colonial 'invention' that involved ascribing monolithic identities. According to Vail (1993), these were key in preventing the appearance of detribalized natives of whom white colonialists were deeply suspicious.

Where indirect rule was most prominent, a local oligarchy was often subsumed and made reliant upon the metropole. It was through these autocratic, but mostly respected, organs of power that the will of the colonial administration was imposed. In some cases, such as with the Lozi of Barotseland and the Baganda of Uganda, the internal political structure of the nation was left virtually untouched except that traditional rulers were now answerable to a narrow, white, elite layer of authority. This authority was invariably located in a remote European-style new urban place such as Lusaka, or an adapted African urban place created for colonialist economic expediency. So long as value, usually in the form of taxes combined with migrant labour, was seen to be exacted from these rural regions, the colonial administration exempted itself from the need, impetus and expense of extending formal colonialism to peoples and regions not deemed economically viable.

Thus, through the cooperation of traditional leaderships, colonial regimes were able to withhold modernizing influences applied in the colony area from other parts of the country, sowing the seeds for future mistrust and intergroup rivalry. This is at the root of much of the inter-ethnic rivalry in Nigeria, where first Yorubaland in the south-west and then Iboland in the south-east benefited from educational, professional and commercial opportunities, while in the north, which received none of these, Britain found willing allies for their system of indirect rule in the Fulani emirs (Bartkus 1999). That traditional rulers and colonial overlords seemed able to coexist and cooperate so well can be ascribed to the fact that both existed as the most powerful echelons of their societies, which were highly stratified by class. Both were used to occupying and articulating power and status.

The same dichotomous power relations between urban and rural populations continued when colonial rule gave way in the second half of the twentieth century to rule by African nationalists from the urban centres; they also inherited from the departing colonial regimes whatever institutional capacity was left behind. The towns, cities and whatever industrial development existed were much easier to imbue with republican and African nationalist sentiment. Urban populations could more easily be deracialized and democratized. Here we can equate 'democratize' with the taking on of citizenship along the lines of the Greek city-states, where those in the countryside were considered as backward and less developed. Urban bias quickly set in, encouraged by the modernization thinkers and strategists of the day and as the new governments also realized that their constituencies lay in the towns and cities. Meanwhile, in the rural areas, most of which the colonialists had not bothered to penetrate (with the obvious exception of settler agricultural areas) or had kept under control using the sway of traditional leaderships, contestation over political allegiances soon began to emerge.

As in the case of the Lozi, sharp differences soon emerged between the all-encompassing ideals of nationalism and the threat that this posed to traditional leaderships and authority. Nationalist politicians encountered difficulties in mobilizing rural people and their leaders through dynamics such as deracialization, which was rarely an issue in the countryside, and democratization, which was perceived as threatening the status quo of traditional authorities. This sometimes resulted in outright conflict or it simmered beneath the surface amid an atmosphere of suspicion and innuendo. Traditional leaders were portrayed by the nationalists as backward and reactionary, holding up the spread of modernity to the rural masses. The former colonial powers mostly supported the new nationalist governments; they left former polities that they had used to their advantage in indirect colonial rule at the mercy of nationalist regimes that felt little empathy towards traditional rulers.

The colonial economies

Looking back at the 1920s and the 1930s, it is difficult to escape a certain surprise at the general ease with which the imperial powers retained control over the colonial possessions in Africa. Indeed, and despite what we will say below about centralization, the colonial system was in some respects very tenuous, dependent upon quite limited numbers of European personnel. For example, the whole of Nigeria, with a population of around twenty million, was administered by 386 colonial civil servants (1:54,000 of the population); there were 4,000 soldiers and 4,000 police, of whom only around 150 were British. In French West Africa, the ratio was 1:34,800; in the Belgian Congo, 1:27,500 (Post 1964). In Mozambique, the colonial administration was even more remote, with parts of the country being administered by concession companies (Newitt 1981).

By the 1930s, the pre-colonial economic structures had been remodelled into a series of colonial economies with distinct characteristics. The common element was that they were all concentrated on production of foodstuffs and raw materials for metropolitan processing and consumption. In turn, they reimported processed commodities. The development of infrastructure reflected the extractive nature of these economies. There were three main patterns:

The West African (found also in Uganda) – involving the incorporation of peasant farmers (Nigeria: groundnuts, Ghana: cocoa, Uganda: coffee and cotton).

The Equatorial/central/southern pattern – company-owned plantations using forced/waged labour – oil palm, rubber in Congo, Angola, Mozambique, and to some extent in Tanganyika, sisal. Also associated with mining in some places (Katanga, copper).

The settler pattern – white settlers using wage labour (Southern

Rhodesia). However, there were variations in this pattern depending upon whether or not the white settler interests were considered paramount. Thus in Congo, Mozambique and Angola, European settlers combined with concession companies and their interests were paramount; in contrast, in Kenya, Côte d'Ivoire and Northern Rhodesia, African interests were not unprotected.

These differences had implications for how decolonization was possible. Thus, in the areas where concession companies and settlers were least important (Gold Coast, Nigeria, Upper Volta, Senegal), independence came easiest. Contrast these areas with Southern Rhodesia and Mozambique, where white settlers and companies fought to protect their interests. In all areas, however, few African rural people remained unincorporated into the world economy with forced labour and peasant production of cash crops. The effects were the development of a rural sub-proletariat associated with the plantation, labour migration and the development of an urban proletariat in mining areas. As labour was diverted from food production in these areas, so other areas had to compensate and become surplus-producing. In these areas, often of smallholding production, new forms of rural social differentiation began to develop. We see this continuing to have an impact on current challenges to food security and access to land, as will be explored in detail in Chapter 3.

The whole system functioned on the conviction that the administrator (the white European) was sovereign and that their subjects neither understood nor wanted self-government or independence. Indeed, such were the ambiguities in which rulers and the ruled were involved, they were generally only vaguely, if at all, aware of them. If there was any training and adoption of the native, it was a schooling in the bureaucratic toils of colonial government; a preparation not for independence, but against it. It could not be otherwise. Colonialism was based on authoritarian command and, as such, it was incompatible with any preparation for self-government. In that sense, every success of administration was a failure of government. With good reason, then, both Africans and Europeans usually approached problems of governance circumspectly.

Inheritance at independence

The Second World War had a profound impact on colonizers and colonized alike, setting in train a series of developments that led to the rapid dismantling of the European empires. Once war began, the Western Allies' claim that the basic issue was freedom versus tyranny had a meaning to Africans that the Allies had not entirely foreseen. In particular the Atlantic Charter (1941) forged by American president Franklin Roosevelt and British prime minister Winston Churchill promised self-determination for all people. The war also revealed and increased European weaknesses. In 1940, Nazi armies crushed France in a lightning campaign, occupying most of the country and reducing the rest to a dependency. Even more stunning, Japan inflicted a devastating series of defeats on British forces in the Far East the next year, shattering for ever the Europeans' myth of their inherent superiority over the rest of humankind.

The end of the war left the metropolitan powers exhausted and weak. More fundamentally, and as Basil Davidson rightly noted, 'the war gave a new spur to anti-colonial protest' (Davidson 1964). It brought a new force to the call for anti-colonial change, and the war experience helped to develop a better resistance to colonial rule. By the end of the war, although African colonies were still economically dependent on their colonial powers, the latter's political and social control was weakened beyond repair. Indeed, this pattern was evident across the colonial world. The Dutch tried holding on to Indonesia, as the French tried in Indochina and subsequently in Algeria, by massive force and at disastrous cost. The sporadic troubles of the British Empire, previously put down by punitive expenditure, were tending to grow into prolonged guerrilla wars. In the African case, the result was a cascade of constitutional formulae and bargaining processes, which eventually culminated in the emergence of native-rule states on the continent.

Though independence brought an extraordinary opportunity to establish something resembling the Hobbesian social contract in Africa, in truth it was severely flawed (Zartman 2005). Studies of particular colonial records show that it is very difficult to trace any continual preparatory process at work, or any sign of a prepared policy until after the Second World War. Even then the post-war years were too late for preparation, save as a purely political, almost desperate, effort to provide an ideology of delay (in the granting of independence). The notion of preparation was to justify the colonial record, as a tactic of delay in the sense that 'you would not seem to be delaying, only training and educating' (Busia 1967). The Theory of Preparation 'emerged after the event', Lord Hailey (1961), a British colonial administrator, agreed. A decade after the end of the war, he wrote that there was no training machinery of administration ready to hand.

In this sense, the real political inheritance of the African elites at independence were the authoritarian structures of the colonial state, an accompanying political culture and an environment of politically relevant circumstances tied heavily to the nature of colonial rule. Imperial rule from the beginning expropriated political power. Unconcerned with the needs and wishes of the indigenous population, the colonial powers created governing structures primarily intended to control the territorial population, to implement exploitation of natural resources, and to maintain themselves and the European population for all European colonizers. British, French, Belgian, Portuguese, German, Spanish and Italian power was vested in a colonial state that was, in essence, a centralized hierarchical bureaucracy. In these circumstances, power did not rest in the legitimacy of public confidence and acceptance. There was no doubt where power lay; it lay firmly with the political authorities. Long-term experience with colonial states also shaped the nature of ideas left at independence. Future African leaders, continuously exposed to the environment of authoritarian control, were accustomed to government justified on the basis of force. As a result, notions that authoritarianism was an appropriate mode of rule were part of the colonial political legacy. Ironically, it was ultimately this curious identity of interest between the new elites and the colonial oligarchy which facilitated the peaceful transfer of power to African regimes in most of colonial Africa.

What emerged from the post-colonial agreement, therefore, was above all an agreement between nationalist elites and the departing colonizer to receive a successor state and maintain it with as much continuity as possible (Zartman 1964). Herbst (2000) also makes a very valid point about the agreement being explicitly about how nationalist elites allocate the 'Golden Eggs of independence', not an agreement involving the body politic, as the idea of a social contract implies. Less explicitly, it was also an agreement among the nationalist elite on the allocation of rules, roles and shares in the benefits of independence, not an agreement involving the body politic, as the idea of a social contract implies. Highly explicit was the notion that the nationalist movement turned single party incarnated the nation in its social, political and economic form; deeply implicit was the promise that the nationalized state would provide the population with the benefits that the colonizer had enjoyed and more, through jobs and services; when the golden eggs ran out, the goose was nationalized and distributed. However, no popular accountability was provided. The only accountability was to the military, and the replacement of nationalist elites by their military only locked the closed door of accountability.

When all that was left of the goose was bones, the nation demanded accountability of the state. Indirect taxation of agriculture, rent-seeking, corruption and poor management, over-indebtedness and falling terms of trade invalidated the old contract (ibid.). The collapse of ideological supports for party–state monopolies at the end of the Cold War and their replacement with notions of political and economic competition set the stage for new terms. However, full political and economic participation and political and fiscal accountability have taken hold, even imperfectly, in only a few places (Zartman 1997: 36–48). Instead, the second wave of democratization of the 1990s petered out on most of the continent, leaving only unsubstantiated forms of accountability and a population repeatedly disenchanted and alienated by rent-seeking elites. Instead of serving as the manager of conflicts and the arbiter of demands among various demand-bearing groups in society, the state has become the source of conflict with such groups and the repressor of their demands.

In the first decade of the new millennium, the appearance of a new social contract is still a development in waiting. Accountability that had appeared in many states in the 1990s then stagnated in either a Tweedledee–Tweedledum alternation or a one-step progression from a single party to a dominant party (*un parti quasi-unique*, in French-speaking Africa). Often, ethnic or atavistic rebellion made the system a bi-party or 'quasi-federal' state. Nations fractured into acephalic segmentary systems where none had existed before. Inefficiencies and structural adjustment limited state functions and state capacities. A third wave of state collapse has not materialized but widespread state failures have occurred. These conditions will be assessed in the following sections. Yet the African state continues to exist, perhaps held together in the end by a lack of alternatives.

State of Africa

There is a growing consensus on what the key elements of governance reforms in Africa should comprise. These include creating or strengthening institutions that foster predictability, accountability and transparency in public affairs; promoting a free and fair electoral process; restoring the capabilities of state institutions, especially those in states emerging from conflicts; anti-corruption measures; and enhancing the capacity of public service delivery systems. Nothing better illustrates Africa's commitment to a new approach to governance than the establishment of the African Peer Review Mechanism (APRM), under the aegis of the New Partnership for Africa's Development (NEPAD). Created as an instrument to which African governments voluntarily subscribe, the APRM has developed agreed codes of governance and incorporated a mechanism for review of adherence. About half of African countries have acceded to the APRM and several are nearing completion of their first review. The APRM is not intended to be an instrument for coercive sanctions, but a mechanism for mutual learning, sharing of experiences and identifying remedial measures to address real weaknesses. Thus, the periodic evaluation built into the APRM process will help governments address obstacles that hinder effective governance in their countries.

Critical to improving the quality and efficacy of the public sector is commitment to public service capacity-building. Capacity-building entails several components of which three are critical: namely training, funding of civil service modernization, and adequate pay for public servants. Deterioration in these areas has adversely affected the ability of the public sector to deliver services, and this theme is returned to throughout Chapters 3, 4 and 5. Indeed, inadequate levels of African salaries have been a major cause of weak incentives, high turnover and corruption. In many African countries, this has led donors to support expanded employment of expatriates. Although intended to compensate for weakness of national expertise, the practice uses up a significant proportion of aid resources without developing national capacity. United Nations (UN) studies have shown that it would be both cheaper and more sustainable if part of the aid budget were used, for an interim period of several years, to support national salaries, strengthen incentives and build national capacity on a sustainable basis. This would help African countries develop the expertise to manage their development programmes. Thus, one area in which international support should be aligned with African efforts is providing funding for these three critical dimensions of public service capacity-building.

In reality, four patterns are evident. First is the emergence of dominant party systems, in which opposition parties serve as safety valves or weak and ineffectual symbols of 'good governance', unlikely to come to power. This is Botswanan democracy, much touted for its freedom, but far from the test of alternation frequently proposed (Stedman 1993; Bauer and Taylor 2005). The same applies to Tanzania. The second pattern, an evolution from the first, limits the degree of change even when alternation occurs. Either the opposition coming to power ends up acting with the same corruption, cronyism and control as its predecessor, or it is replaced by the predecessor after a single turn, or the reality of change in the nature of the state is over. The first was the evolution of Senegal, Kenya, Zambia; the second in Benin benevolently, and Congo-Brazzaville violently.

The third pattern, partially overlapping some aspects of the other two, is the category of unreconstructed authoritarian regimes embodying the ethos of the previous civilian and military single-party regimes with only symbolic nods to the rising procedural demands, including, variously, Guinea, Togo, Congo-Brazzaville, Gabon, Chad, Burkina Faso, Rwanda, Eritrea and Angola; a motley assortment. The fourth category includes some arguably promising unknowns, whose seemingly positive multiparty experience is recent enough to warrant suspended judgement, including Sierra Leone, Liberia and Congo. The relation of such a categorization to the nature of the African state is complex. From this summary, it is hard to assert a winning dynamic in any of Africa's regions that would tip it in the direction of full satisfaction of procedural demands for meaningful participation in the state. The dominant party system, the first pattern and its evolution, and the second pattern are functionally little different from the single-party system, with the exception that the latter has the softening feature of a safety-valve opposition to relieve pressure on the dominant/single party.

The ensuing model of the state is then one of an authoritative institution supported by a vertical column of the population, heavy at the top and charged with its own justification and legitimization rather than being emergent and supported from the base. Those not in the column are excluded from the system of allocating benefits and excluded from the allocation of benefits as well. An excellent study by Kayizzi-Mugerwa (2003) shows that African states privatized 'only when the [politicians] were sure that the benefits to themselves and their supporters exceeded the costs, including loss of rents, of denationalization' despite the opposition of 'the local middle class' and public opinion in general. When elections are not decisive, open, programmatic contests, private interests take over. '[R]egimes have sought to protect the interests of a narrow stratus of state elites and have regularly been willing to inflict austerity on the population' (Van de Walle 2001: 16), a situation that the evolution from single- to dominant-party regimes, with or without alternation, has not changed. As an institution responsible to its stockholders, the state is above all beholden to its board of directors and only secondarily to its other shareholders, including multinational corporations, bilateral and multilateral donors and the international financial institutions.

Of course, this picture depends on the assumption, or the evidence, that the single/dominant party is a weak mobilizer, involving a limited column of supporters in a passive role, a description that generally obtains across the continent. One result of this situation is the outbreak of two types of endemic conflict, both of them voicing the complaint of the excluded. One is a centralist conflict for power without any programme to distinguish rebels from government. This is the time-at-the-trough phenomenon, whereby one group – often without any inscriptive or other distinguishing characteristic other than simply being excluded – seeks to replace the other in the seat of power without any clear ideological or programmatic difference. The conflict bears no procedural demand; it simply voices a substantive demand for me rather than for you. Thus rebellions such as the Revolutionary United Front (RUF) in Sierra Leone or Renamo in Mozambique were not ethnic revolts, and their programmatic elements were tenuous.

The other is a regional or ethnic revolt for self-determination, voicing deeply procedural demands to take the governing process into its own hands because those in power have shown that they cannot be trusted to allocate benefits fairly. Such are the rebellions of the Democratic Forces Movement in the Casamance in Senegal, the New Forces in the North in Côte d'Ivoire, the Acholi through the Lord's Resistance Army (LRA) in Uganda and the rebels in Darfur and Beja in Sudan, among others. Still others bridge the two categories; they are not content to seek self-determination for their region, but rather want their turn to govern everyone (as in the first type), but for the defence of their own ethnic group. Such were the Tutsi of the Rwandan Patriotic Front (RPF) and now the Hutu of the Democratic Forces for the Liberation of Rwanda (FDLR).

The frustrated shift from substantive to procedural demands in the 1990s has meant that that nature of the African state is still uncertain at a crucial junction. At the beginning of the shift it was torn between the pressures for change and the obstinate reality; in the middle of the first decade of the 2000s, pressures remained in violent conflicts, but slumped into alienation and indifference in the general public. The demands for pluralization, accountability and participation have produced results in form, but not much of a change in the nature of the state, from a delegated to a participatory democracy.

Conclusion

At one level, looking back, one may see now that the colonial period was no more than a single episode in the onward movement of African life. In another sense, it was an unexampled means of revolutionary change with its dramatic and lasting effects on the continent, its people and their history. In truth, the extension of European empires had mixed motivations. The people with whom the Europeans came into contact responded in different ways, as their own political necessities and values dictated. The impact of European expansion, therefore, is a complicated equation, being a function both of European motivation and African response. The consequences of those differential impacts are crucial to any understanding of the complexities of contemporary African politics and society.

In the end, none of these positions helps us to understand what is happening in Africa. In the twenty-first century, changes in the world order, the failure of statism as a strategy, the existence not only of an economic but also of a political crisis in Africa, make the careful study of a continent that contains 13 per cent of the world's population of great importance. However, as a background to this study, we must recognize that there is also an intellectual crisis on the continent today. The old panaceas of African unity and African socialism seem to have failed. The intellectual analysis from within Africa of what is to happen and of what has happened is merely the beginning. For the moment, structural adjustment policies are dominant, and the old dictators (Mengistu, Kaunda, Moi, Banda, Mobutu) have gone, but where this all leads and what African intellectuals are making of it are not at all clear.

TWO
Instabilities, adjustment and renewal

Africa has become the third world of the Third World – a continent beyond the pale of the dominant movements of the 21st Century [...] and [...] with the exception of South Africa and Nigeria, if it were to disappear in a flood the global effect would be approximately non-existent. (General Olusegun Obasanjo, cited in Poku and Mdee 2010)

Africa's rapid transition to independence, if it made the early 1960s heady with optimism, left a damaging legacy of myth and illusion. Independence came to be seen by too many as a single act, like running the new national flags up the flagpole. To the elite, independence was reduced to a constitutional formula in which they contested the terms and indemnities for the departing power. The departing power was intent on handing over political power only as long as this did not affect their economic stake. In all cases the political elite saw independence not as the beginning but as the end in a process of change. However, the colonial forms of governance were deeply flawed. The political inheritance at independence was models of governance wholly imported from Europe and imposed on societies that could scarcely be less like those for which they were prepared. In the end, the assumptions of the imported systems proved untenable in the new states. Nothing illustrates this more than Africa's economic decline.

By any measure, the vision of prosperity espoused by the liberating leaders, such as Kwame Nkrumah of Ghana, seems no more than a distant dream from which one has awoken to another historic epoch. This is an epoch in which the Millennium Development Goals (MDGs), set in the year 2000 by the global community to halve poverty and hunger, arrest diseases and environmental degradation, help newborn babies survive infancy and educate them in childhood by 2015, will not be met in post-colonial Africa (Poku and Whitman

2011). Across the continent, domestic economies remain fraught with a wide range of problems, many of which have existed since the 1960s, but which have been compounded with the passage of time. Despite decades of structural adjustment pressures and related external and internal remedies, the promised advantages of economic restructuring have not been borne out: foreign investments have failed to flow in; the debt burdens have continued; and commodity prices go on fluctuating amid declining industries. As regards links with the global economy, dependence on external resources, even for budgetary support, continues to increase, but the actual flows have fallen short of requirements.

Africa's economic decline

By the early 1980s, the symptoms of Africa's economic malaise were evident almost everywhere on the continent. The returns on investment by organizations such as the World Bank were much lower in Africa than in other regions. It was, and still is, impossible for Africa to attract foreign private capital, either in investment or loans, and portfolio investment flows were negligible (see Table 2.1). The international price for Africa's government debt in secondary markets was the lowest for developing countries, reflecting the markets' perception of the continent as not creditworthy. The physical infrastructure, already poor, deteriorated from lack of maintenance, and the quality of government services declined, fuelling, among other things, civil discontent and corruption.

Unable to borrow to finance domestic expenditure, governments on the continent were forced to turn to the International Monetary Fund (IMF) and the World Bank (WB) for support. The IMF and the WB quickly identified domestic policy weakness as the main culprit in accounting for the continent's dire economic position – in particular, the continent's debt burden. To be clear, debt is not intrinsically bad. Households borrow to smooth consumption or for large purchases such as a car or house. In many countries, economic development has historically been financed by capital inflows, including loans from governments or private banks, to finance infrastructure development and other large investments. What matters is that a country has the capacity to repay. If the debt burden is too great then there can be a number of negative repercussions for economic and social develop-

TABLE 2.1 Foreign direct investment (as percentage of global FDI flows), 1997–2010

Indicators	1997	1998	1999	2002	2007	2010
Developed countries	56.8	69.8	77.2	79.1	80.1	
Developing countries and economies	39.2	27.2	20.7	18.9	18.0	
Asia	22.4	13.8	9.3	11.3	11.2	
Latin America	14.9	12.0	10.3	6.8	6.8	
Africa	2.3	1.2	1.0	0.7	0.7	
Africa (as a percentage of developing countries)	5.88	4.63	4.72	3.78	3.87[1]	3.11[2]

Notes: 1. UNCTAD data, 2010; 2. UNDP data, 2010
Source: ADB Statistics Division and IMF

ment. Debt service uses up foreign exchange (forex) from export earnings, so there is less forex available for imports that are necessary for growth and may be essential for social welfare, notably medicine. Since the government is responsible for paying nearly all developing-country debt, the payment also takes away from the amount available to provide services or undertake investments. Furthermore, the theory of debt overhang suggests that private investors will also be deterred by a country's large debt burden.

The proximate causes of Africa's debt crisis are well known, but bear repeating: they are an outcome of weak leadership and poor advice during the first decade of indigenous rule. Although it is currently fashionable to suggest that the economic troubles of the continent began with independence, this is not entirely true. African economies performed relatively well in aggregate terms between 1960 and 1970. During this period, gross domestic product (GDP) and exports grew at rates comparable to those in the other main developing regions and more rapidly in general than those in South Asia. Most notably, manufacturing production rose at sustained rates, although from very low levels and in sectors such as food processing, textile, construction materials and other simple consumer goods, which employed relatively unsophisticated technologies (see Table 2.2). Enthused by a permissive international climate with an avid appetite for raw material

TABLE 2.2 Selected macroeconomic indicators, sub-Saharan Africa and South Asia, 1963–80

Macroeconomic indicators	Sub-Saharan Africa		South Asia	
	1963–73	1973–80	1963–73	1973–80
GDP	6.0	2.8	3.7	4.3
Agriculture	2.2	0.0	3.4	2.4
Manufacturing	10.7	10.2	4.1	5.2
Export	16.9	−0.6	−0.7	5.8

Source: World Bank, *World Development Indicators*, Washington, DC, 1989

from Africa, post-colonial leaders embraced the notion that rapid development was possible through intense industrialization.

For indigenous leaders, independence was an opportunity to demonstrate not only their qualities as human beings, but also their competence as state managers. Nkrumah offered the following insight: 'with self government, we'll transform Africa into a paradise in ten years' (cited in Wallerstein 1961: 11). Nkrumah's optimism derived from his unshakable faith in the dominant development theories of the day: modernization and industrialization theories. Promoted by Western development experts and embraced uncritically by post-colonial leaders, both theories held that the new nations should continue to focus on exporting raw material to industrialized countries in order to finance their own rapid industrialization programmes. Inspired by the successes of the Soviet Union in the 1930s, they envisioned the rapid development of basic industries within a socialist structure of central planning, with commitment to science rather than magic or religion as the appropriate vehicle for consolidating change.

Across the continent, post-colonial governments drew up five-year plans, created public enterprises and enacted regulations to control prices, restrict trade and allocate foreign earnings in pursuit of social goals (Poku 2006). At the same time, countries were struggling to establish themselves as nations and put effective governmental structures in place. However, the strategy of rapid industrialization was deeply flawed as governments became overextended, particularly relative to their weak institutional base, as they tried to build national unity and deliver on the promise of independence. Robert H. Bates

(1981), in an insightful volume, has adequately documented the dire consequences of a too-rapid plunge into industrialization for societies that are basically agricultural. Bates concludes that 'the costs of rapid industrialization are placed largely on the backs of the diminishing pool of agricultural producers'. After increasing by 2.2 per cent between 1963 and 1973, agricultural exports declined to negative figures by the late 1970s (see Table 2.2).

The Yom Kippur War of 1973 was to have a particularly deleterious effect on the continent's development strategy. The war resulted in the Organization of the Petroleum Exporting Countries (OPEC) agreeing to a dramatic increase in the price of crude oil on global markets. Given the importance of oil to the fledgling industrialization on the continent, the OPEC decision severely depleted the continent's reserve of foreign exchange while simultaneously increasing their already heavy burden of debt as they attempted to continue to maintain imports of petroleum necessary for continuing their economic development plans.

So, how much debt are we talking about, both in relative and absolute terms? Accuracy in figures relating to aggregate debt is notoriously difficult to obtain, but using various sources it is possible that, at the beginning of the 1980s, sub-Saharan Africa's external debt stood at US$203 billion, equivalent to $758 per person, compared to the region's average income per person of just $470 (United Nations 2001). Although this figure is quite modest by global standards – Brazil, for example, owed more than $120 billion at the end of 2008 – compared to the continent's ability to repay, this debt is enormous. Africans can pay off the debt only with earnings in foreign currency, so they must use money from exports, from aid or from new foreign loans. Thus, Ethiopia's debt of $10 billion ($179 per person) at the end of 1996 may not seem like much compared to the $19 billion Europe spent on ice cream in 2009, but the $10 billion debt was almost thirteen times the amount the country earned in exports in 2009 ($783 million), and debt repayments were the equivalent of 45 per cent of these export earnings.

There is another important difference between Latin American and African debt. While most of Latin America's debt is owed to commercial banks, most of the debt owed by African nations is to official donors and multilateral organizations such as the World

Bank, the IMF and the regional development banks. For low-income countries – defined by the World Bank as those with per capita gross national product (GNP) below $785 – multilateral debt increased by some 544 per cent between 1980 and 2000, from $24.1 billion to $155 billion, as credit from other sources dried up and repayments mounted. Multilateral debt constitutes 33 per cent of the long-term debt burden of the most impoverished countries (ibid.: 165). For middle-income countries, the corresponding percentage is 15. Neither agency is permitted, under existing rules, to reschedule or write off debt; and repayments to both have to be met in full.

The growing importance of the IMF and the World Bank as creditors has made debt management less flexible. As more and more Third World countries ran into greater difficulties servicing the huge loans made to them by Northern banks and multilateral institutions in the 1970s, pressure to adopt structural adjustment policies (SAPs) grew strong as a wide range of bilateral and multilateral donors insisted upon economic reform as a condition for the disbursement of funds and for rescheduling the debt. By the end of 1985, twelve of the fifteen debtors designated as top-priority – including Argentina, Mexico and the Philippines – had submitted to structural adjustment programmes (Debt Crisis Network Staff 1985). Over the next seven years, Structural Adjustment Loans (SALs) proliferated as the economies of more and more Third World countries came under the surveillance and control of the World Bank and the IMF. Cooperation between the two institutions was brought to a higher level with the establishment in 1988 of the Structural Adjustment Facility (SAF) to closely coordinate both institutions' surveillance and enforcement activities.

Although there were many variations of SAPs at country level, at heart they all shared the same logic: namely the need to maintain fiscal discipline while discouraging protectionism. Implicit was the assumption that post-colonial development, with its heavy emphasis on state-led development, had failed Africa (Collier and Gunning 1999). Structural adjustment, therefore, was designed to roll back the state: privatize public enterprises, dismantle trade barriers, abolish state marketing boards, remove price controls, and liberalize exchange rates.

These measures were meant to help countries resolve balance-of-payments problems, reduce inflation and to prevent future economic crisis by promoting longer-term structural reforms, particularly those pertaining to the public sector. Often they led to periods of economic austerity as government expenditure was slashed and market forces were unleashed. The World Bank euphemistically called this process 'crossing the desert', and argued that short-term pain was necessary for long-term success in economic growth and improvements in the quality of life (Stewart 1995). The 'short-term pain' provoked a storm of criticism, especially from African governments and non-governmental organizations (NGOs). They were joined by international agencies such as the United Nations Children's Fund (UNICEF), which in 1987 made a fundamental challenge to the adjustment paradigm by publishing *Adjustment with a Human Face* – a multi-country study of the effects of IMF policies on children. In response, both the World Bank and the IMF said they would prioritize the social sectors and poverty reduction concerns in their policies and even admitted that their initial attempts in the early 1980s to push through adjustment, whatever the price, had caused unnecessary hardship.

Yet the main policy thrusts of adjustment programmes remain in place today and both the IMF and the WB still tend to maintain that, where programmes fail, it is because of inadequate implementation on the part of national governments. In truth, however, it is not clear whether the lack of effective implementation results from African governments' unwillingness to undertake reforms or from the objective conditions of the economies not permitting the kind of adjustment being recommended. Despite nearly two and a half decades of adjustment policies, this debate remains largely unresolved. The only certainty, however, is that SAPs often have an immediate and, at times, detrimental impact on the welfare of the poorest members of society, especially as they affect food prices, costs of education and payment of medical services. Riley and Parfitt (1994) argue that the overall result of such economic policies is often 'to destabilize the recipient states as key groups in the populace rebel against the combination of rising prices and declining real wages and public services'.

The Heavily Indebted Poor Countries (HIPC) initiative was launched in 1996 by the IMF and the World Bank as a response to some of the difficulties noted above. The main purpose of the HIPC was the reduction of eligible countries' external debts to sustainable levels, thereby creating the basis for achieving debt sustainability and sustainable economic growth. The initiative was enhanced in 1999 to provide faster and deeper debt relief to a larger number of countries. Under the HIPC initiative, a country that successfully demonstrates a satisfactory track record in implementing sound macroeconomic policies and achieving predefined structural reform and poverty reduction objectives (HIPC trigger points) is to have its net present values of debt reduced to 150 per cent of exports or 250 per cent of government revenue. The HIPC initiative was presented as the most comprehensive debt relief effort coordinated by the international community to date and involved for the first time relief from multilateral creditors.

Under the Initiative, thirty-eight low-income countries (LICs) could potentially qualify for debt relief. Of these, twenty-seven countries reached their decision points as of August 2010, and are benefiting from debt relief. These countries account for 85 per cent of total relief expected to be provided under the HIPC initiative. Twenty-four of these countries were African and have reached their completion points, and so are now receiving all debt relief committed under the initiative unconditionally and irrevocably. On average, and combined with other bilateral debt relief, the overall debt stock of the twenty-four countries that are now receiving HIPC relief would be reduced by about two-thirds; and their debt service relative to exports is being lowered by about one third to below 10 per cent, or less than half the average for other developing countries. However, the HIPC initiative is not meant to be a permanent mechanism and ensures the reduction of a country's debt stock only at a point in time. It, alone, cannot ensure that debt sustainability will be maintained in the future. Maintaining debt sustainability over time is a complex undertaking that will require countries to consistently pursue sound economic policies, good governance and obtain new financing on appropriate terms. For many countries, the latter requirement may oblige them to seek an increase in the level of concessionality of their financing.

The countries of sub-Saharan Africa, with their poor credit rating, have largely been turned into an IMF/World Bank 'macroeconomic guinea pig' since they depend greatly on resources from the multilateral institutions. Out of the total of forty-seven countries in the region, thirty were implementing adjustment programmes in 1999 jointly administered by the World Bank and the IMF. Whereas the number of IMF stand-by arrangements declined from a high of

132 in the 1981–85 period, to forty-nine in 1996–98, the number of enhanced structural adjustment facilities (ESAFs) grew from eighteen in 1986–90 to a record high of ninety-nine in 1991–95, and ninety-six in the 1996–98 period (International Monetary Fund 1998). Very high proportions of ESAFs were with the countries of sub-Saharan Africa. Since most of these countries have very weak political structures, an IMF–World Bank condominium has been imposed on them under the guise of providing aid. As a result, these countries have pretty much ceded their sovereignty to the IMF and the World Bank (Mkandawire and Soludo 1999).

The hard economic statistics confirm what the television coverage of Niger's famine in 2010 suggests: the African crisis is deep and enduring. Each year, the World Bank categorizes the 198 or so states of the world on the basis of their economic development and performance. The numbers in each category vary from year to year, but roughly forty states in the years between 1990 and 2010 were designated as low-income countries – these are countries with high population growth rates, low income, low literacy and low life expectancy. In 2010, some 80 per cent of countries in this category were African (United Nations Development Programme 2009). There are only eleven African countries in the middle category – Algeria, Botswana, Egypt, Gabon, Libya, Mauritius, Morocco, Namibia, Seychelles, Swaziland and South Africa – six of which have a combined population of just 5.6 million – Mauritius, Namibia, Seychelles, Botswana, Gabon and Swaziland. The remaining forty-one countries on the continent are in the low human development category. This, however, does not tell the entire story. There are fifty-five countries in this category, which means African countries account for 85 per cent of the category. Even more telling is that, of the thirty countries with the lowest human development indices, twenty-six (or 89 per cent) are African.

Not surprisingly, poverty has increased at a faster rate on the continent than anywhere else in the world. With a fifth of the world's population, the continent is home to one in three poor persons in the world, with four of every ten of its inhabitants living in what the World Bank classifies as 'a condition of absolute poverty' (Minujin and Delamonica 2003). The poverty of these nations is confirmed by other basic indicators, such as production capacity and performance, and trade imbalances; aid, debt and capital flows; food and agricultural production; fiscal data; and various social indicators pertaining to longevity, infant mortality and medical services. During the 1990s the region experienced a decline in GDP per capita of 0.6 per cent per annum and, because economic growth was highly skewed between countries, approximately half the total population was actually poorer in 2010 than they were in 1990. It is also the case that income and wealth distributions are extremely unequal in many countries and, with improved growth rates, such inequalities are likely to increase rather than to diminish (Easterly 2009). The resulting social decay presents a dramatic picture of insecurity of ordinary people in circumstances where states, and the international system of states, are either unable to provide protection or are themselves the principal sources of violence, as is further explored in Chapter 5. If we remove territorial boundaries from our cognitive map, we are left with an image of people across the continent deprived of their basic needs in conditions of extreme adversity as state managers either fail to generate, or appear incapable of generating, a stable platform for economic development.

The latest economic indicators from the *African Development Report 2010* underline the extent of Africa's decline. The report's celebrated headline growth of 3.3 per cent in GDP in 2009, compared to 3.0 per cent in 2008, belies the systematic decline observable in real per capita GDP growth from 1.0 per cent to 0.8 per cent in the same period (United Nations Development Programme 2010: 8). In developmental terms, this means that the combined economies of Africa actually shrunk by 0.2 per cent in the twelve months up to the end of 2009. To put this in context, all other regions in the world are already outperforming Africa, and efforts to redress this poor performance since the 1970s have not been successful. In 2009, for example, the average GNP per capita in the Organisation for Economic Co-operation and Development (OECD) countries was $28,086, compared with $528 in Africa. This means that the industrialized countries are roughly fifty-one times wealthier than African states. Assuming that the OECD countries could stop stretching this development gap further, and hoping that African economies could grow at an annual rate of 3.5 per cent over the coming years, it would take the continent some 135 years to reach today's level of wealth enjoyed by OECD countries.

The colonial legacy

Concerns about the nature of Africa's economic decline usually focus on greed and grievance, with their associated corruption, nepotism and violence. It is not difficult to see why; Africa is a continent where incompetence, materialism and the lust for power have unleashed untold violence on ordinary men and women. Until recently, coups of the elite type were the most common way of changing national leadership; civil wars spawned the largest refugee population with one of every two Africans being a homeless victim of war (Fosu and Collier 2005). The political norm was near-absolute power in the hands of political leaders who, with few exceptions, tolerated no opposition, rigged elections and regarded the revenues of the state as personal income. Yet to reduce the lack of development progress since independence to this series of calamitous events and processes merely serves as a framework through which analysts are able to politicize Africa's difficulties without adequate analysis of the available facts – i.e. context and history. In truth, there is a confluence of factors ranging from poor policies at both macro and micro levels to the corrosive effects of colonial legacies on economic and political systems over time.

The period of European occupation in Africa can be viewed in two different ways. From one point of view it was an interruption in the development of African history, a development governed by social forces originating within the continent itself. In this view, the new states, which rapidly succeeded the old colonial possessions, can be regarded as legitimate successors of the states and cultures whose process of development was interrupted (Fieldhouse 1986). The second view sees the new states as the successors rather of the colonial powers, with the nature of their institutions and political life, as well as the economies upon which these depend, directly determined by the colonial system that went before. It is not necessary to accept either of these views in its entirety, though each gives valuable insight into the nature of modern African states. However, there can be little doubt that the impact of the colonial powers upon Africa was enormous and the colonial legacies enduring.

Nothing illustrates this more clearly than the colonial legacy on African economies. Under colonial rule, African colonies were required to specialize in the production of one or two commodities.

The colonies were usually not competitive with each other, and the production of commodities was complementary to the industrial needs of the colonial powers. At best, production was sufficient to provide both a revenue and an employment base for the particular colony. Thus, Ghana specialized in cocoa; Tanzania in sisal; Sierra Leone in iron ore; Zambia in copper; Malawi in tea; Uganda in coffee and cotton; and Nigeria in peanuts, palm oil and rubber. The departure of European powers along with colonial collapse left the new states exposed as virtually single-commodity economies, leaving them extremely vulnerable to the vagaries of international commodity markets with not inconsequential effects on the continent's overall economic development.

Since the late 1960s, Africa's importance as a supplier of raw materials (which in many African countries still generate up to 90 per cent of export earnings) has diminished with competition from synthetic substitutes from other regions of the world. Thus, between 1967/68 and 2006/07, Africa's share in global primary product export declined by half, from 8.3 per cent to 4.2 per cent (UNCTAD 2006). During the 1990s, short periods of price recovery were superimposed upon a relentless downward trend. By 2005, real non-oil commodity prices had fallen to less than half their 1988 levels (World Bank 2008). In the case of tropical beverages such as coffee and cocoa, the decline was even more severe than the average, with prices falling by almost 70 per cent (ibid.: 7). Translated into financial returns, the cumulative losses suffered by developing countries amounted to $290 billion between 1990 and 2004 (Maizels 1994). For sub-Saharan Africa, the most seriously affected region, the loss was equivalent to 5 per cent of GDP.

Commodity market fluctuations provide another example. In 2009, the international price for copper was around $2,600 per tonne. Evidence that an individual trader in the Sumitomo Corporation, one of Japan's big five *soga shosha* (Japanese international general trading firms with integrated and coordinated services and production), had been attempting to drive up the price through future trading on the London Metal Exchange led to a spate of panic selling that drove the price down to $2,000 per tonne in less than one month (*The Economist*, September 2010, p. 31). For Sumitomo, the episode translated into a loss of $1.8 billion. That sum is equivalent to over half of the GDP of Zambia, which derives more than 80 per cent of its export earnings from copper (ibid.: 31). For Zambia, the collapse of copper prices translated into foreign exchange losses of around $150 million – more than the level of government spending on health and education combined (ibid.: 31).

The negative effects of the characteristic price volatility of primary commodities have been compounded by a decline in their terms of trade. Terms of trade declined by 24 per cent and 21 per cent respectively for North and sub-Saharan Africa between the early 1970s and the late 2000s. This secular decline has been an important reason for the continent's marginalization in world trade. According to the United Nations Conference on Trade and Development (UNCTAD 2010: 35) a significant part of the decline in the share of sub-Saharan Africa in world exports since the early 1990s can be explained by the fall in the prices of African products relative to the rest of the world. For sub-Saharan Africa it is estimated that if the terms of trade had stayed at the level achieved in 1980, its share of world exports today would have been almost twice as high. Africa's current share of world trade is a story of lost potential earnings and resultant damage to the lives of millions of its citizens. 'For African countries that are not oil exporters, and excluding South Africa, cumulative terms of trade losses in 1970–1997 represented almost 120% of GDP, a massive and persistent drain of purchasing power' (World Bank 2005). These resource losses have been an important element in the region's poor economic performance since the early 1980s. UNCTAD (2006) has estimated that the availability of these resources would have raised Africa's investment ratio by almost 6 per cent in non-oil-producing African countries and added 1.4 per cent yearly to annual growth. This would give a per capita GDP of $878 for 2006 instead of the actual level of $323. In other words, if non-oil exporters in Africa had not suffered from continued terms-of-trade losses in the past three decades, the current level of per capita income would have been higher by as much as 62 per cent.

The export trade figures encapsulate the lives of millions of Africans: the millions of smallholder producers who account for the bulk of Africa's export agriculture; the millions of rural inhabitants whose livelihoods and environment have been devastated by the oil and non-fuel mining industries that loom large in the continent's exports; and the millions whose opportunities never arose because of the resource drain. These people exert little influence on the domestic and international factors and forces that determine commodity prices and thereby shape their lives. For example, coffee prices were at an all-time low in 2010, devastating the lives of millions of coffee-producing families, but not the business of the big firms that control the international retail trade in processed coffee. Between 2001 and 2009, coffee prices fell by two-thirds and the price paid to farmers in Tanzania fell from $1 per pound in weight to 28 cents. This was 9 per cent of the USA retail price of roast and ground coffee. At the end of the chain, the beverages giant Nestlé, one of the four companies that control the coffee world, is estimated to make a profit of at least 26 per cent on each cup of its instant coffee (Rajan 2010).

Political legacies

Analogous to economic legacies are political legacies and their effect on Africa's economic development. The nature of the African state in particular has been a significant barrier to political stability, a key prerequisite for economic stability. As we noted in Chapter 1, the colonial powers did not seek to build nations, with some combination of cultural, linguistic and patriotic unity, as was the case in Europe. Instead, the African states emerged from the authoritarian structures of their colonial past. Consequently, the parallelism between statism and nationalism has had a limited role in contemporary African politics, making the Hobbesian social contract difficult to formulate on the continent. There is ample evidence that post-colonial leaders tried to rectify this problem. In some states, the dominant traditional nation became the core of the new nation, as other ethnic groups were assimilated into it or marginalized. Wolof in Senegal, American-Liberian in Liberia, Hutu in Rwanda, Shona in Zimbabwe, Baganda in Uganda and Amhara in Ethiopia were the key elements in defining the new nations as the cultural basis of the new state (Clapham 1990). In other states, an artificial creation was decreed and all traditional nations were dissolved in it; those who could or would not fit were excluded. The *Ivoirité* of President Henri Konan Bédié defined a new nation of essentially southern ethnic groups 'native' to the land within Côte d'Ivoire's boundaries and the rest were decreed non-nationals and non-citizens.

Yet in all these cases the social experiment failed to produce a unified nation upon which a strong state could be built. Partly the failure derives from an inability to construct 'constitutive stories', such as those associated with a 'freedom struggle' that are inappropriate to large sections of the population who did not participate in, or understand, such dynamics, although they were all impacted by them. In such situations, people, particularly in the rural areas, receive or are 'subjected' to citizenship that they have not chosen and of whose value they are not convinced, simply because they, or their community, happen to live where a new state was born. As R. M. Smith (2002: 109) asserts, 'Even today [...] most people acquire their political citizenship through unchosen, often unexamined, hereditary descent, not because they explicitly embrace any political principles [...]'

Consequently, state power has never rested on the legitimacy of public confidence or acceptance. Instead, it has resided firmly within political authorities or patronage. This has given rise to a position where individuals have greater attachments to their localities (or local communities) than to the overarching state (Rothchild and Victor 1983). Hence, though the notion of the state is accepted, the political institutions through which its powers are exercised are treated with remarkable indifference. Until recently, multiparty systems have been replaced by single-party states, and in turn by military regimes, without raising much more than a flicker of interest from any but those who were immediately affected by the change. For the great majority, life simply went on and, while passive acceptance of this nature certainly has much to be said for it, it provided no assurance of political stability and no more than a resigned and probably temporary acquiescence in whatever policies the government pursued.

State effectiveness has, therefore, continually decreased as a result of ongoing use of political power for private gains by African leaders. Resource allocation by government and other state institutions has often come to follow ethnic or religious lines and in many states is heavily influenced by external actors (Herbst 2000: 233). Owing to an absence of effective structures with autonomy and strength to check corruption, the governing elite of most African states have engaged in high and sometimes egregious levels of corruption. In countries such as Nigeria, Sierra Leone, Democratic Republic of Congo, the Central African Republic and Zimbabwe, corruption is so extensive

TABLE 2.3 Deaths from conflict, 1963–2008

Country	Years	Estimate of war deaths	Battle deaths	Battle deaths as percentage of total war deaths
Sudan (Anya Nya rebellion)	1963–73	250,000–750,000	20,000	3–8
Nigeria (Biafra rebellion)	1967–70	500,000–2 million	75,000	4–15
Angola	1975–2002	1.5 million	160,475	11
Ethiopia (not including Eritrean insurgency)	1976–91	1–2 million	16,000	<2
Mozambique	1976–92	500,000–1 million	145,400	15–29
Somalia	1981–86	250,000–350,000	66,750	19–27
Sudan	1983–2002	2 million	55,000	3
Liberia	1989–96	150,000–200,000	23,500	12–16
Democratic Republic of Congo	1998–2001	2.5 million	145,000	6

Note: Non-battle deaths are due mainly to war-exacerbated disease and malnutrition

Source: United Nations (2009: 24)

that it is viewed as a way of life. Making or receiving bribes is considered a practical method for supplementing one's interest and achieving economic security far in excess of individual ability. An unpublished report from the United Nations examining corruption in fifteen African countries suggests that nearly 40 per cent of annual government budgets are misappropriated by corrupt governing elites in the most affected countries (Poku 2006).

Across the continent, the necessity to earn income is strong, exacerbated by poverty, by low and declining civil service salaries and lack of social protection. Those who are in work are under severe pressure to provide for the extended family, in the absence of any state safety nets. Opportunities to engage in corruption are numerous (Blundo and Olivier de Sardan 2006). Monopoly rents can be very large in highly regulated economies. In transition economies, economic rents are particularly large because of the amount of formerly state-owned property that is essentially up for grabs. The discretion of many public officials is also broad, and this systematic weakness is exacerbated by poorly defined, ever-changing and poorly disseminated rules and regulations. Accountability is typically weak. Political competition and civil liberties are often restricted. Laws and principles of ethics in government are poorly developed, if they exist at all, and the legal institutions charged with enforcing them are ill prepared for this complex job. The watchdog institutions that provide information on which detection and enforcement are based, such as investigators, accountants and the press, are also weak.

The segmentation of society that has followed has impeded the many reforms of the political structures that could possibly have enhanced Africa's ability to develop sustainably, as well as exacerbating political tensions on the continent (McGowan 2003). The obvious manifestation of this is the litany of conflicts strung across the continent. Between 1970 and 2008, more than forty-two wars were fought in Africa, with the vast majority of them intra-state in origin. In 2008 alone, fourteen out of the fifty-three countries of Africa were afflicted by armed conflicts, accounting for more than half of all war-related deaths worldwide and resulting in more than eight million refugees, returnees and displaced persons – see Table 2.3.

Where violence is central to political processes, and even more so when it is ideologically legitimized, the basis for civil politics is profoundly endangered. Violence has its own dynamic. As Clausewitz famously pointed out, war tends towards the absolute. There is probably no war in modern history that has achieved its 'aims' without, at a minimum, either grossly compromising itself in the process, or creating a legacy that has subsequently undermined the victory. Even when violence is not actually used on a day-to-day basis, militarized forms of governance have a similar logic, which is towards a concentration of power, towards values that promote hierarchy, obedience, command and decisive action, and devalue democracy, dissent, consensus and patience. Violence incubates religious, ethnic and political extremism on both sides. Violence promotes a hegemonic masculinity. It is when the threat of violence is lifted that we can begin to envisage civil politics dominated by debate, argument and consensus.

Although the causes of Africa's many conflicts are well documented, their effects on the continent's economic development have been less so (Collier 1999). Yet the rampancy of these events has not been benign to Africa's economic growth or development (Martin-Prével et al. 2000). Conflicts affect the economy through reduced investment in both physical and human capital, as well as through the destruction of existing assets, including institutional capacity, and these are reflected in reduced economic growth. Statistics show that countries that experienced a civil war had an average income that was about 50 per cent lower than countries that did not experience a conflict, and investment ratios for both physical and human capital were also about 50 per cent lower in conflict countries. Conflicts across the region have profoundly changed the social welfare of affected societies as military spending has diverted increasing proportions of national resources from pressing developmental needs. Local and national economies have suffered huge output losses with devastating consequences for the quality of life as populations became poorer. Conflicts have led to widespread dislocation of populations and loss of household savings.

The marginal functionality of governments in countries torn by years of internal fighting, and the erosion of essential service structures, foment inequalities, grievances and strife, and perhaps most importantly, pervasive human insecurity on a regional scale, as currently exists in much of the African Great Lakes region and in the Horn of Africa (ibid.). Against such backgrounds, the prospects for a transition from war and organized violence to 'post-conflict' environments are difficult to achieve and sustain; and even non-violent 'normality' (which, in the worst cases, is outside of lived experience) is often not sufficient for human welfare on a scale that could credibly be described as peaceful. Expressed bluntly, 'for good or bad, war has been an engine of change, and it is dangerous to assume these changes away in any plans for reconstruction' (Keen 2005: 27). Table 2.4 below indicates the key features that are generally regarded as typifying the phases of transition from violent conflict to a post-conflict condition.

A study by Wallensteen and Sollenberg (2001) finds that war and underlying risk factors are the reasons why low-income countries, and Africa specifically, failed to catch up to the slower-growing developed countries. The poorest countries have lost, on average, some 40 per cent of their output through greater frequency of war compared with the rest of the world (Collier et al. 2004). Wars alone explain almost the entire relative decline of the less-developed countries (LDCs) compared with the middle-income countries. In other words, had prevalence of war among LDCs been at the same level as elsewhere, the LDCs would have at least kept pace with the rest of the world.

Exports may be particularly vulnerable to political instabilities. The evidence is clear that African exports have not performed well since the 1970s, especially when compared to exports from developing countries generally. Fosu (1991) reports results showing that not only has conflict adversely affected export performance in sub-Saharan Africa, but also that the impact on export growth is substantially higher in magnitude than on GDP growth. Specifically, the effect of a unit change in an index of three types of coup events would result in a reduction of GDP growth of 0.3 per cent per year, compared with a decrease of 1.0 per cent for exports. The estimated partial elasticities are 0.35 and 0.73, respectively. That is, a 10 per cent increase in political instability would lead to a decrease of 3.5 per cent in GDP growth, but as much as 7.3 per cent in the rate of growth of exports. The relatively large export impact may be attributable to the competitive nature of exports coupled with the tendency for political instability to raise the inefficiency and cost of production (ibid.). It seems reasonable to infer, therefore, that political instability was a significant reason for the historically dismal performance of exports, and by extension GDP growth, in Africa.

TABLE 2.4 Conflict to post-conflict environments – key features

Environments	Conflict	Transition from conflict to peace	Post-conflict
Security	Armed conflict is ongoing in most or some parts of the country. Civilian police and other law enforcement institutions may not be functioning throughout the territory. Violations of international human rights and humanitarian law.	Violence in many forms may continue in most or some parts of the country. Peace support operations start filling the security vacuum where needed. Violations of human rights start diminishing.	Law-based and accountable control of military forces. Growth in perceived legitimacy and effectiveness of civilian police. Elimination of warlordism; reduction in organized crime.
Political	War mentality and effort prevail. Armed forces and groups are powerful. State institutions are weak.	'No peace no war' situation. Politicization of armed forces and armed groups starts: they begin to familiarize themselves with democratic governance. State institutions start becoming more legitimate and effective.	Introduction, extension or reinforcement of participatory democracy. Standards of good governance established. Enfranchisement of previously marginalized and/or hostile groups.
Social	Loss of human capital and population displacement. Disruption of community networks and traditions. Public social services are often unavailable.	Rebuilding of human fabric begins. Individuals start overcoming trauma; communities start rebuilding social cohesion. Essential social services start being restored (education, health, water and sanitation).	Decline of pernicious forms of identity-based politics. Restoration of sociocultural norms, local and national. Human and capital investments in anticipation of long-term peace and stability.

| Economic | Infrastructure is often damaged. Markets collapse and unemployment is widespread. Local communities and civil society develop alternative coping mechanisms to fulfil basic needs. Informal sector economy grows. | Infrastructure rehabilitation begins. Local and national economic recovery begins. | Formal markets resume and expand; trade links are re-established. Employment prospects improve. Growth of formal economy and viable tax base. Government-funded/-facilitated social services expand and strengthen. |

Source: Adapted from ILO, *Prevention of child recruitment and reintegration of children associated with armed forces and groups: strategic framework for addressing the economic gap,* International Labour Organization, Geneva, 2007, p. 20

Conclusion

Well after the first flushes of excitement in the immediate aftermath of decolonization – when it seemed possible that movements of national liberation might overthrow colonial regimes along with their pervasive legacies – it is generally accepted that colonialism did not die so quick a death after all. Instead, it has become increasingly clear that colonialism lived (and lives) on in many forms and ways. Most obviously, colonial rule had political and economic effects that have been captured, at least in part, by the terms 'neocolonialism' and 'neo-imperialism'. The political instability of many new nations was clearly the result of a multitude of infrastructural problems, ranging from the enormous chasms separating colonial elites from the populace to the myriad divisions that had often been carefully engineered by colonial regimes precisely to retard the political development of nationalism. Similarly, economic underdevelopment was widely seen as the result of limited colonial investment and the continuation of marked disparities in access both to capital and markets between the formerly colonized and their colonizers.

But even in the most scathing of early critiques, the depth of the disparities, and the continued commitment of new (and old) 'colonial' institutions to political and economic dominance on a global scale, was hardly anticipated. Furthermore, perhaps as significantly, the extent to which the impact of colonialism was social and cultural, as well as political and economic, obscured both the prospective durability of colonial forms of dominance and the many ways in which colonialism lived on in the categories and procedures of knowledge itself. In retrospect, Fanon's notion of renovating violence, that real freedom for Africans could be won only by destruction, and true liberation only through fire, has proved to be an ultimate perfidy (Fanon 1961). Violence in Africa has begotten more violence. The outcome is the culture of corruption, brutality, destitution and despair, the many facets of which we have discussed in this chapter.

THREE

Food-insecure and vulnerable: the politics of African rural livelihoods

With little time left to make significant progress before 2015, it is unlikely that the first Millennium Development Goal, to eradicate hunger and poverty, will be achieved in Africa. In the longer term this will be achieved only with a more robust global strategy to create sustainable livelihoods, which not only ensure the 'right to food', but also create systems of food production that can feed growing and increasingly urbanized populations in the context of climate change and diminishing oil reserves. On a regional level, the previous chapter has emphasized the problematic and unsustained nature of economic development on the continent. This chapter develops from that starting point and argues that the political and economic marginalization of rural livelihoods and agriculture has been a theme in both colonial and post-colonial regimes.

Africa is still predominantly rural (although rapidly urbanizing), but development strategies have suffered from a decidedly 'urban' bias. The necessary investments in rural infrastructure, education and health, which would be inherently pro-poor and pro-growth, have been lacking, being deemed politically unimportant. This has undoubtedly contributed to the slow reduction in poverty in most African economies. Even some of the recent and much-trumpeted economic growth in some countries has often been based on sectors such as tourism and mining that have a minimal impact on the reduction of poverty. This chapter therefore attempts to present a comprehensive and political engagement with rural livelihoods and, specifically, the role and development of agriculture. However, agriculture should not be viewed in isolation; it is not only a significant productive activity in rural Africa, but is a crucial component of most rural and many urban livelihoods that combine on-farm and off-farm activities. It is likely and desirable that fewer people will rely on agriculture as productivity increases, as they become better educated and are able to take up other opportunities for employment and enterprise. Subsistence and small-scale agriculture is unstable and highly vulnerable, yet it is a key contributor to the livelihoods of the majority of Africa's population. Without significant investment in appropriate education, infrastructure and technology, this is the situation in which most Africans will remain.

Levels of hunger and poverty in Africa would almost certainly decline through improved local and regional agricultural production. The majority of the population of sub-Saharan Africa remains dependent on agriculture as a key component of their livelihoods. Therefore, increasing the productivity and sustainability of agriculture is a fundamental challenge. However, the challenge of agriculture in Africa is by no means a new one. Colonial and post-colonial administrations sought to revolutionize and control peasant agriculture through the creation of large plantations and settlement of lands. There was a general belief that agriculture would be modernized, commercialized and export-led as the newly independent states progressively industrialized. However, in much of the world, and particularly in sub-Saharan Africa, fully modernized agriculture remained an elusive small-scale goal and family farmers have continued to feed the bulk of the population (Ponte 1999; Wiggins 2009). Aid funding and government spending on agriculture declined from the 1980s onwards, with many agricultural research and extension institutions and subsidized input schemes scaled back. The state was no longer to be the agent of modernization in agriculture, but the market would drive commercialization and productivity gains.

Global agriculture now faces a double challenge: climate change and increasing energy costs. Climate change is predicted to have severe impacts on agriculture in Africa and, while we cannot predict exactly the scale and substance of such impacts, it is likely that increasingly erratic weather patterns will disrupt the livelihoods of farmers dependent on rain-fed agriculture. This will have major social impacts that can already be seen in increasing conflicts over land and natural resources (Toulmin 2009).

At the same time, energy costs are rising and global food production systems are responsible for a significant proportion of carbon emissions. Predictions suggest that, in the coming decades, oil reserves will decline and will push the cost of energy ever higher, as the consumption habits of an expanding global population increase demand. Current global food systems are energy intensive in the form of inputs (agrochemicals and fertilizers) and in fuel for transportation. In 2008, oil prices reached their peak and food prices also increased, resulting in riots in a number of countries. Inflation in the price of basic food commodities had a significant impact on poor consumers, who spend large proportions of their income on food.

There is now a general recognition that the future of food and agriculture requires radical rethinking (Rao 2009; Woodhouse 2009). In sub-Saharan Africa, donors and governments have begun to reconsider agriculture as a significant component of poverty reduction. The role and persistence of small-scale farmers were formally recognized by the World Bank in the 2008 *World Development Report*. However, there is significant debate in relation to the strategy that sub-Saharan Africa should adopt for the improvement of food production systems.

Some see the answer in technology in a new green revolution that enhances agricultural productivity through genetically modified (GM) crops and agricultural modernization (Collier et al. 2008; Gowing and Palmer 2008). However, there is fierce opposition to this perspective, which argues that GM crops will further reinforce the marginalization of small farmers and threaten biodiversity. A growing movement seeks a more radical transformation through heavily localized food production systems with increased use of organic and low-input agriculture.

This chapter, therefore, seeks to highlight a number of key areas in this debate. It begins by charting investment and support for agriculture in Africa and considers the prospects for current initiatives. It then considers access to land and access to inputs, both of which are crucial in developing small-scale agriculture. Sub-Saharan Africa is currently the focus of significant levels of land grab, as wealthier countries seek to ensure their own food supplies. The issue of whether or not to subsidize agricultural inputs is also a focal area of debate. We explore the case of Malawi, which is seen to provide important lessons for the continent and indeed challenged the assumptions of donors and the international financial institutions. The chapter then goes on to explore issues around increasing the resilience of small-scale farmers and considers the role of agriculture in productive and sustainable livelihood systems, with the consequent implications for the roles of internal and external actors. It is mistaken to assume that all of these questions are technical; the history of agriculture in Africa and the issues outlined above are deeply political in relation to the just and effective allocation of resources and to the possibility of a less vulnerable future for the majority of Africans.

The state of agriculture in sub-Saharan Africa

Agriculture in sub-Saharan Africa (SSA) remains dominated by smallholder farmers. It is estimated that 56 per cent depend on agriculture for their livelihoods in total with 69 per cent living in rural areas, and 86 per cent of these depend on agriculture, but also supply the urban areas (Hazell et al. 2007; Jazairy et al. 1992; Rockström 2003; World Bank 2009). It is important to qualify this with the recognition that agricultural and food production activities cannot easily be divided between individuals who might be labelled as 'farmers' and 'non-farmers'. Agricultural activities are often combined with off-farm activities as part of a diversified livelihood, which enables households to reduce their vulnerability to external shocks and stresses such as droughts or floods (Ellis 2000). Not only is SSA heavily reliant on agriculture, it is also the only region in the world where poverty and undernourishment have been increasing over the past twenty years and where those living on less than US$1 per day have become poorer (Staatz and Dembélé 2007).

This poverty remains a strongly rural phenomenon. SSA also has the largest proportion of ultra-poor people who live on less than $0.50 per day (International Food Policy Research Institute 2009).

The majority of the sub-Saharan African population depends to some extent on small-scale agriculture for food and livelihood. However, the significance of agriculture does not necessarily reveal itself in economic indicators, as most producers operate at the margins of the formal economy and commercial markets. Estimates vary substantially as to the contribution of agriculture to gross domestic product (GDP). One report (Integrated Regional Information Networks 2009) suggests that 40 per cent of GDP in SSA relates to agriculture. However, the Food and Agriculture Organization of the United Nations (FAO) suggest that agriculture contributes 15.6 per cent to GDP in all Africa and 16.4 per cent in SSA. There is also a substantial range in the contribution from 54 per cent in Central African Republic, to 1.6 per cent in Botswana. Further, it is estimated that agriculture employs about 80 per cent of the total workforce (Integrated Regional Information Networks 2009). However, levels of food insecurity have remained roughly constant as a proportion in recent decades with around 32–35 per cent of the sub-Saharan African population classified as undernourished (ibid.).

As populations have continued to increase in real terms, in 2005 the number of undernourished people was estimated to be 200 million, an increase from 131 million in the early 1990s (Food and Agriculture Organization of the United Nations 2008).

The reasons for the lack of adequate food for individuals and communities alike are multiple and are certainly not determined solely by production of agricultural products. Social and political entitlements to land, water and inputs also shape access to agriculture and, similarly, to consumption of the products. However, in SSA, where the majority of the population depends to some degree on agriculture, productivity gains are likely to have a significant impact on food consumption. It is argued that the failure of African agriculture can be attributed to declining donor and governmental investment in agriculture. For example, it is estimated that global financial assistance for agriculture declined from $6.2 billion to $2.3 billion between 1980 and 2000, to the advantage of other sectors (Mkandawire and Albright 2006). Consequently, agricultural production in the sub-region has declined owing to farmers' inability to purchase the necessary agricultural inputs. For example, in Zambia, farmers have shifted from production of maize and other nutritious and income-generating crops to cassava and millet, which require less fertilizer (Leavy and White 2006). Table 3.1 shows the slow rate of progress of agriculture in SSA over a forty-year period and illustrates the low level of inputs

TABLE 3.1 Development of sub-Saharan African agriculture

	1962	2002
Irrigation (%)	2.47	3.95
Modern seed (%)	0	24
Fertilizer per hectare (kg)	2.9	13.1

Source: Food and Agriculture Organization of the United Nations (2009: 51)

considered key to increasing productivity. In the same period, fertilizer use and productivity in China has increased dramatically. In one study it was shown to reach 588 kilograms per hectare as opposed to 7 kilograms in Kenya, with China's use considered excessive and Kenya's inadequate (Stanford University 2009).

According to the *Africa in Our Hands* report (Africa Monitor 2009) food security and hunger tops the concerns of the poor, for it is agriculture on which they depend for daily survival. Yet productivity in agriculture in SSA has been stagnant for three decades and is the lowest in the world. The report takes testimonies from Kenya, South Africa, Chad and the Gambia, which show that the most significant challenges to productivity are climatic factors, lack of access to agricultural inputs and access to land. Farmers themselves blame the liberalization of the sector and removal of subsidies, plus high demand, which has pushed the prices of inputs to high levels.

External factors and global food prices

An argument often made in relation to African agriculture is that production subsidies in Organisation for Economic Co-operation and Development (OECD) countries unfairly block exports from Africa, and certainly imports from such countries have disrupted local markets by flooding them with cheap produce (Holt-Giménez and Patel 2009). However, according to the FAO, African exports are only 2.4 per cent of production, and it therefore makes more sense for Africa to look to the development of regional markets to support substantial growth in the agricultural sector. Wider external challenges to the global food system such as increasing energy prices may also limit the potential and desirability of export-led growth (United Nations Food and Agricultural Organization 2009; Holt-Giménez and Patel 2009). In addition, Africa is currently disproportionately dependent on food aid with 17.1 per cent imported in 2009 (United Nations Food and Agricultural Organization 2009). Stronger productivity and regional markets in Africa could reduce this dependency.

With a rapidly increasing urban population, rising food prices are significant. Global food prices doubled between 2005 and 2007 and continued to rise to mid-2008 (see Figure 3.1).

The reasons for the price spike included droughts in key regions, low stocks of cereal/oil seeds and feedstock being used in biofuel

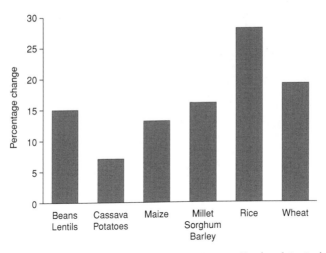

FIGURE 3.1 Increase in food prices 2006–08 (*source*: Food and Agriculture Organization of the United Nations 2009)

production, alongside increasing oil prices and the decline of the dollar (ibid.). All of these factors are likely to recur in the future as a result of increasing climate change and increasing energy prices. It might also be argued that increasing food prices are also an opportunity for African farmers to get better returns from their products, but again, at present, this is limited by the chronic problems in agricultural productivity and lack of robust marketing institutions and mechanisms. The FAO uses the example of Uganda, which showed no production response to price rises. Farmers are not able to respond to the market in this way, as land is in small parcels and they have little access to credit inputs. Government invests only 1.5 per cent of national expenditure in agriculture and there are few farmers' organizations to enhance bargaining (ibid.).

It is broadly agreed that African governments have, in recent decades, failed to make the necessary commitment to agriculture. In 2003, signatories to the Maputo Declaration from the African Union endorsed the New Partnership for Africa's Development (NEPAD) Comprehensive Africa Agriculture Development Programme (CAADP) and promised to allocate 10 per cent of government expenditure to agriculture. The data from 2007 suggested that only six countries spent 10 per cent or more (Ethiopia, Senegal, Mali, Malawi, Zimbabwe and Burkina Faso), with the mean spend being around 5.5 per cent, and seventeen countries spent less than 5 per cent (see Figure 3.2). According to the CAADP website, some progress, albeit slow, is being made, and in 2010 some eleven countries committed to spending 10 per cent (Comprehensive Africa Agriculture Development

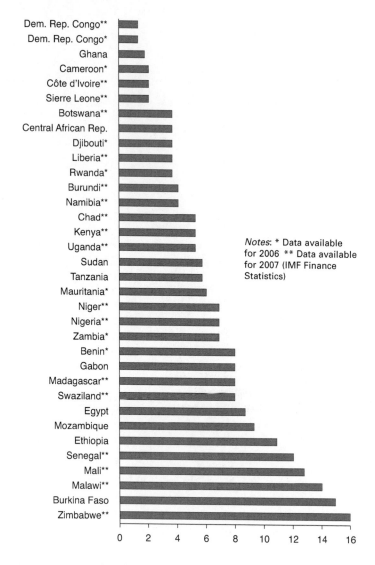

Notes: * Data available for 2006 ** Data available for 2007 (IMF Finance Statistics)

FIGURE 3.2 Agricultural spending by selected African countries in 2008: percentage of total government expenditure (*source*: Africa Monitor 2009: 38)

Programme 2010). Billed as an 'African-owned' initiative, CAADP is built around four pillars: land and water management, market access, food supply and hunger, and agricultural research. Emphasis is placed on improving the availability of agricultural inputs and addressing rural infrastructure shortages, promoting sustainable land management and improving access to appropriate technology, as well as building an African common market for agricultural products.

The CAADP sets some ambitious targets – for instance, the commitment to ensure food security by 2015 - and yet in 2009, 30 per cent of children remained underweight on the continent (Africa Monitor 2009).

The *Development Support Monitor*, which takes a broad and longitudinal view of agriculture, suggests that some countries are performing well in improving smallholder agriculture, such as Nigeria, Malawi, Rwanda and Sierra Leone. However, many other countries are yet to make significant progress in either increasing productivity or in ensuring access to food. One country that stands out in terms of both approach and results is Malawi, a country that has increased agricultural productivity, particularly for small-scale farmers, through strong leadership by government-targeted financial disbursements, a pro-poor agricultural policy and improved technology. We will return to the case of Malawi later in the chapter.

In addition to direct investment in agriculture, there are also a range of consumption, producer and trade-oriented interventions that African governments are currently implementing both to stimulate productivity and ensure access to food. For example, Egypt, Senegal, Ethiopia and Lesotho have introduced food subsidies, Cameroon and Senegal are implementing price controls, Ghana and Rwanda are offering producer support, and Benin, Burkina Faso, Liberia and Malawi have export controls and reduced import subsidies (United Nations Food and Agricultural Organization 2009). None of these measures is particularly radical and all have been used in the past, particularly in the immediate post-colonial period, but under liberalization they were discouraged (Griffiths 2003).

We have noted above that African governments have been criticized for failure to support agriculture, and the same argument is also directed at international donors. The last decades also saw large declines in aid to agriculture, with aid flowing into other sectors. Figure 3.3

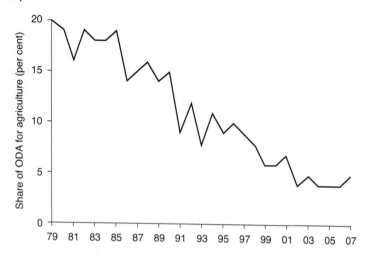

FIGURE 3.3 Share of ODA for agriculture (*source*: United Nations Food and Agriculture Organizaton 2009: 12)

shows that at the close of the 1970s, 20 per cent of Overseas Development Assistance (ODA) was directed towards agriculture, but by 2003 this had fallen to below 5 per cent (around $2.3 billion). However, donors have promised to reverse the decline of ODA to agriculture, and by 2007 spending on agriculture had risen to $4.2 billion (ibid.). The European Union (EU) pledged to support CAADP in 2007, and now a range of donors have committed to support a CAADP multi-donor harmonization fund under the control of NEPAD (Comprehensive Africa Agriculture Development Programme 2010).

It would be a mistake to think that donors and the wide range of external actors with an interest in African agriculture are in agreement concerning the fundamental challenges that it faces. While it can be argued that the World Bank's recognition of the importance of small-scale farmers is positive, critics argue that actually the *World Development Report* offers little in terms of how the change will be achieved beyond that the World Bank will retain a market- and private-sector-led growth strategy and will seek to support farmers in diversifying their livelihoods and finding exits from agriculture (Rao 2009; Woodhouse 2009). Aid remains largely focused on the macro level, while there is a growing consensus among large donors that more effective aid should have an emphasis on food production, food security, agricultural and rural development. The emphasis on food production is a welcome evolution, but the expectation that markets and private-sector-led growth will lead the transformation seems to ignore decades of evidence to the contrary. For example, the FAO highlights the case of Uganda above, which dismantled many of its publicly funded agricultural support mechanisms such as extension services under the Plan for the Modernization of Agriculture (PMA) with the expectation that the private sector would fill the gap. It did to some degree, but served only the needs and interests of wealthier commercial farmers (Muhumuza 2002; Woodhouse 2009).

Partnerships with the private sector do have a potentially important role to play, but cannot replace public intervention, particularly for small-scale farmers, and a range of partnerships are now evolving (with parallels to those now targeted at HIV/AIDS). In 2007, the United States Agency for International Development (USAID) put $7.7 million into the West African Seed Alliance with inputs from global seed giant Monsanto and the Bill and Melinda Gates Foundation.

There are increasing calls for an African green revolution starting from the better use of natural resources, but also incorporating the use of modern technologies such as GM seeds. New and influential donors such as the Gates Foundation see answers to the chronic productivity problem in technology (Gates Foundation 2009). USAID also favours genetic engineering, but the FAO, the OECD, the United Nations Conference on Trade and Development (UNCTAD) and the International Food Policy Research Institute (IFPRI) caution that this should be appropriate and targeted at needs of the poor population (UK Food Group 2008: 26).

An increasingly vocal and growing global movement urges a more fundamental resistance to such technologies, arguing that they will damage biodiversity and place too much control over production in the hands of a few large companies (Holt-Giménez and Patel 2009). Research and agricultural support has tended in the past to neglect subsistence agriculture, and it is argued that technological 'quick fixes' ignore the complexity and social aspects of agricultural livelihoods. The UN's International Assessment of Agricultural Knowledge, Science and Technology for Development (IAASTD), published in 2008, which took four years to produce and included the inputs of more than four hundred consultations, found GM had contributed little to eradicating hunger and argued for a more agro-ecological approach.

This conclusion has proved unpalatable to the green revolution lobby, and these conclusions have largely been ignored by influential actors such as the World Bank (ibid.).

Hunger and food security in Africa are far more than an issue of increasing productivity, and an agro-ecological approach can indeed be very helpful in enabling an improved understanding of the challenge.

Hine et al. (2008), in their report on the potential contribution of organic and low-input agriculture in East Africa, argue that the main factors contributing to food insecurity in Africa are:

- Availability of food – incorporating lack of access to and rights to food.
- Natural capital – degraded natural resources and mono-cropping (often adopted from colonial and modernization projects).
- Social capital – poor collective action and public institutions.
- Human capital – lack of education, poor health and labour, gender issues.
- Physical capital – poor infrastructure and lack of access to technology.
- Financial capital – poverty and lack of access to markets and investment capital.
- Other external factors – land tenure, political issues.

A substantial set of challenges is contained in this list and solving them is not simply a matter of technological inputs (although they are also important). Hine et al. argue that global evidence on more sustainable and less input-dependent agricultural systems shows that such methods can be more productive than commercial mono-cropping systems. Such systems are knowledge intensive rather than resource intensive, and therefore would require far higher investment in agricultural extension and education.

Who owns the land?

Competition for land is growing, with expanding demand to feed expanding urban populations and to grow biofuels, leading to rapid increases in land prices and a pressing need for governments in Africa to clarify and regulate issues of land title in a way that will benefit longer-term food security and resilience to climate change (Toulmin

2009). Devereux et al. (2008: 70) noted that 'the links between land ownership, poverty and hunger among rural people are clear and undeniable and action on improving land access for the poor families lies at the heart of fighting hunger'.

Land is also a political problem. The colonial settlement of lands was an injustice to local populations who, generations later, still suffer the consequences of this marginalization, and is a source of conflict in a number of countries – for example, Zimbabwe, South Africa and Kenya.

Systems of access to land and land ownership vary dramatically across the continent and often involve a complex intertwining of traditional and customary rights to land use with legal and individualistic conceptions of ownership. The issue of gender and access to land is a particular illustration of this. Chapter 4 discusses in more detail how the burden of small-scale agricultural production falls disproportionately on women, as illustrated by Figure 3.4.

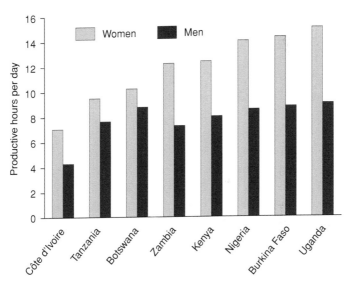

FIGURE 3.4 Rural workload by gender (*source*: Brown and Haddad 1995 in Meinzen-Dick et al. 2004: 9)

In some countries, women work nearly double the hours of their male counterparts. This is supported by Bryceson (1995) and Gladwin (1991, in Wanyeki 2003: 71), who discuss the fact that women work longer hours as they have 'triple responsibilities', working on their own fields, as unremunerated family labour and undertaking domestic labour. However, barely 2 per cent of land in SSA is legally 'owned' by women (Food and Agriculture Organization of the United Nations 2009). Even if many state laws declare that women can own land, customary practice around inheritance may deny women legal title (World Bank 2005; Ellis 2007; Green 2008; Toulmin and Quan 2000; Devereux et al. 2008; Wanyeki 2003; Agarwal 2001; Izumi 1999, Doss 2001; Carr 2008; Peters 2009; Place 2009; Razavi 2007). In many areas of Africa, the idea of a woman having land of her own is an alien concept and one that meets with much resistance. 'Women exist only as the wives of household heads; their actions are considered secondary or unimportant to the changes that landholding systems undergo' (Yngstrom 2002: 92).

When a woman is a widow, single or divorced, if she wishes to acquire land, then more often than not she will be restricted to asking a male member of her family to help her with her attempts to make a claim (Razavi 2007; Place 2009; Carr 2008; Toulmin 2009).

However, to focus simply on a dichotomy between individual title and customary ownership is overly simplistic. Systems of land access are diverse and households may access land using different mechanisms. Woodhouse (2003) argues that increasingly the default mode in Africa has been moving away from customary and collective systems towards individualized and market-based ownership. This has been supported by actors such as the World Bank, which views the ambiguity of customary access to be a barrier to investment and increasing productivity (World Bank 2008). This approach would argue that land ownership also stimulates rural credit markets through giving more marginalized groups collateral to underpin lending for investment.

It is a mistake to see individual land title as a solution to the food security problem; and alternative systems, such as the formation of cooperatives or long-term leasing, might also offer possibilities. In itself, title will not necessarily reduce food insecurity and poverty in SSA, if the size of landholding that is accessed is so small that it prohibits sufficient production. For example, in Ethiopia a large number of plots of land are referred to as 'starvation plots' owing to their size (Staatz and Dembélé 2007). Land title may also be counterproductive; as Davison (1987, in Doss 2001) notes, in matrilineal areas of Kenya, many men will refuse to work on the land of their wives owing to the fact that the land will remain in the wife's lineage and not the husband's. In this instance it could be argued that food insecurity could be exacerbated if husbands are not prepared to contribute to the farm.

Collective ownership and farming certainly has few friends in Africa, the vilification of 'villagization' in Nyerere's Tanzania being a case in point (Scott 1999), with collective farms being blamed for increasing hunger and famines in some areas. In this case, neoliberal myopia and outrage may not be helpful. Socialist Tanzania looked to China for inspiration for the villagization programme. China went on to vastly increase the productivity of small-scale agriculture through an evolution from collective farms through individual access to small plots to state production quotas (Ravillion 2009). Agricultural production in Tanzania stagnated during the same period.

The issue of redistribution of land (often following colonial settlement, but also conflict and political occupation) has been evident in many countries in SSA, most notably in Zimbabwe and South Africa. The overall objective of both countries is to empower the rural poor. However, the manner in which this has been implemented from the perspective of the respective governments is quite different. In South Africa, access to, and redistribution of, land has taken the form of 'willing seller, willing buyer', whereas land policy in Zimbabwe has been 'fast-tracked' to incorporate land invasions and the confiscation of land owned by white farmers. The popular perception is that this has resulted in near economic disaster, devastating agricultural production and increasing hunger. Broekhuis and Huisman (2001), Kinsey (2004), Waeterloos (2004) and Zimmerman (2000) discuss the fact that even with the facilitation of land access for the poor, in South Africa they are ill equipped to endure stresses and shocks and their skills base is limited with respect to agricultural practices. However, more recent evidence from Zimbabwe suggests that this is a myth. Agriculture has to some extent been refocused from large-scale commercial production to a more smallholder-dominated model that has, in a number of areas, shown increases in productivity and sustained investment, albeit under difficult economic circumstances (Scoones 2009; Cousins and Scoones 2009). Controversially, Zimbabwe may actually offer some lessons to the continent in terms of supporting small-scale agriculture. This is not to deny that the confiscation of lands has increased racial tensions and has in part been used as political patronage.

One of the most pressing current political issues in relation to land in Africa is the contentious practice of 'land grab', which may represent an increasing threat to food security for the poorest in SSA. Concerns over the leasing of, or selling of, large areas of land to transnational corporations (TNCs) and external governments by national governments are growing. It is estimated that 2.4 million hectares in Africa have already been appropriated in this way. With arable land and water already in short supply, if land is leased to large-scale farmers and foreign investors, the consequences to local farmers may be negative (Cotula et al. 2009). The effects of land grab have already been felt in Ethiopia, where Rice (2010) notes that many farmers are having their access to water limited owing to the expansion of foreign-owned farms, and their holdings are decreasing. While the risks of this new global acquisition are recognized by the World Bank and IFPRI, it can be argued that their proposed voluntary 'code of conduct' to regulate such deals alongside a fundamental belief in the privatization of land may ultimately increase the dangers of further dispossession and marginalization of the poorest and that more radical and redistributive solutions will be required (Borras and Franco 2010).

Securing inputs for agriculture

Securing access to land is only a part of the food security puzzle; access to inputs to ensure productivity is also crucial. This section will examine the case for subsidies for conventional inputs using the case of Malawi.

Agriculture in developed countries is heavily subsidized, with spending of around $300 billion annually (Lingard 2002; Maene 2000), without which an estimated 40 per cent of EU farmers and their farms would technically go bankrupt (Royal Agricultural Society of England 2000). Such support cannot, however, be found in SSA despite the obvious benefits to resource-poor farmers.

Agricultural subsidies, which were popular in SSA during the 1960s and 1970s, were a casualty of liberalization as donors considered them ineffective and inefficient in transforming African economies (Dorward et al. 2008). Consequently, subsidies have either been eliminated or substantially reduced following the adoption of structural adjustment programmes (Townsend 1999).

Accordingly, fertilizer consumption has declined, resulting in low soil fertility and agricultural productivity (ibid.). Decline in soil fertility is blamed for SSA's slow growth in food production (Sanchez et al. 1997) and deepening food insecurity and poverty. This is because farmers are unable to cultivate high-yielding crop varieties that are also nutrient-demanding. Growth in agricultural production has therefore come from area expansion rather than increase in yields.

However, agricultural subsidy is not without controversy (World Bank 2007; Agricultural Research Institute 2007; Bowers and Cheshire 1983). Sceptics of agricultural subsidies contend that they can distort markets, crowd out the private agricultural inputs market, discourage agricultural diversification and breed corruption (Agricultural Research Institute 2007). Conversely, advocates believe subsidies provide a 'public good' and have social protection benefits for resource-poor farmers, particularly in developing countries (ActionAid 2002). As a social safety net, subsidies play an essential role in resource distribution to disadvantaged groups, poverty alleviation and promotion of long-term growth (Conning and Kevane 2002). Additionally, agricultural subsidies impact directly and indirectly on upstream and downstream industries (Mayrand et al. 2003), thereby generating multiplier effects. It is estimated that the average farm yields in SSA remain at about 1 tonne per hectare (tonne/ha), while maize yield in farm demonstrations is reported to be about 5.2 tonnes/ha (World Bank 2007) leaving an exploitable yield gap of more than 4 tonnes. With most small-scale and subsistence farmers unable to make the required investments in inputs to attain this level of production, the role of inputs support subsidy and investment in rural infrastructure is crucial. It is also crucial to consider evidence that agricultural subsidization of local food production is cheaper, more efficient and effective than food aid (Clay 2006; Sachs 2005).

Malawi, a country of nearly thirteen million, has implemented several Agricultural Input Subsidies Programmes (AISPs) within the last three decades to improve smallholder agricultural productivity, reduce vulnerability to food insecurity and hunger, and stimulate economic growth and development. Some 2.8 million households depend on smallholder farming (Agricultural Research Institute 2007) and agriculture contributes 38.9 per cent of GDP (United Nations Food and Agricultural Organization 2008), 90 per cent of export earnings and over 5 per cent of total employment (Mwangwela 2001), with small-scale farmers contributing 85 per cent of total agricultural production (Nagayets 2005). However, years of neglect and dwindling budgetary support for the Agricultural Ministry and particularly for small-scale farmers has undermined agricultural production, with only 20.68 per cent of the 2,450,000 hectares of total arable land in use and just 3 per cent of it under irrigation (Agricultural Research Institute 2007). Consequently, the country became import dependent, with 30 per cent of the population food insecure (Malawi Vulnerability Assessment Committee 2005) and 34 per cent undernourished (Agricultural Research Institute 2007), with disastrous health and life consequences. Agricultural input prices were high, resulting in 30 per cent fertilizer use at a rate of 4 kilograms/ha (Langyintuo 2005), leading to low soil fertility and poor maize yields of 1 tonne/ha with good rains, relative to the potential of 3 tonnes/ha on healthy soils (Sachs 2005). To address agriculture and food security problems in the country, several policies have been implemented over the years with interesting outcomes. Among them are input subsidies for maize production, despite the country's $113 million national debt (Chinsinga 2008). Support for maize is explained by the fact that the crop is a major staple food of the people (Langyintuo 2005) contributing 58 per cent of the national food basket (Masina 2007); 42 per cent of the total arable land is under maize production nationwide and it is regarded by both the poor and the rich as 'life' (Peters 2006: 328).

The Malawian government has attempted a number of periods of subsidization of inputs for maize production, including the Agricultural Sector Adjustment Programme between 1988 and 1994, which emphasized providing targeted subsidies and improving food crop productivity. This resulted in 16 per cent smallholder agriculture growth and bumper harvests of maize (Harrigan 2003). However, this programme was later abandoned owing to pressure from donors (Chinsinga 2005).

The subsequent implementation of Starter Pack (SP) and Targeted Input (TI) programmes that distributed fertilizers and hybrid maize to rural farming households in the late 1990s, and then following severe drought in 2002 (Peters 2006; Chinsinga 2005), achieved tremendous yield and food security impacts (Agricultural Research Institute 2007; Peters 2006; Blackie 2006), though it is argued that the gains would have been much higher if delays in input distribution and errors had been avoided (Peters 2006). Timely agro-inputs distribution is important to enable farmers to take advantage of available rainfall. Late planting during a particular cropping season can result in the critical growth period of the crop coinciding with the dry spell, which can lead to total crop failure or abysmal yields.

The AISPs have resulted in over a million tonnes of grain surplus above the country's requirement (Integrated Regional Information Networks 2009; Famine Early Warning Systems Network 2009) and lower maize and staple food prices (Integrated Regional Information Networks 2008), thereby benefiting the poor, who spend a great part of their income on maize. A significant increase in casual labour wage rates has thereby impacted livelihoods positively (Chinsinga 2008). The maize surpluses Malawi has achieved from the subsidies have increased food security, with the majority of households now dependent on own production (Famine Early Warning Systems Network 2009). They have improved economic well-being by 8 per cent, and reduced the incidence of household vulnerability from 79 per cent in May/June 2004 to 20 per cent in May/June 2007 (Dorward et al. 2008). For example, according to Famine Early Warning Systems Network's (FEWS NET) December 2008/January 2009 food security update in southern Africa, the population in need of food assistance from January to April 2009 increased by over 24 per cent in Mozambique and 50 per cent in Zambia. However, in Malawi the figure significantly reduced from 1.5 million to 674,000 given a maize stock of 98,377 tonnes to cater for emergencies (Famine Early Warning Systems Network 2009). The food insecurity situation in southern Africa is attributed to high input prices that have limited the land area cultivated by farmers (ibid.). The different situation in Malawi might therefore be evidence of the beneficial impacts of the subsidies targeting resource-poor small-scale farmers. Malawi also benefited from foreign exchange earnings as it was able to sell excess production to neighbouring countries.

Impacts of the AISPs in Malawi suggest that successful implementation of subsidy programmes is possible without donor support even in poor countries if there is political will. This is also the approach being pursued under the Millennium Villages Project, which subsidizes inputs of fertilizers and seed, with beneficiaries expected to contribute a proportion of their production in return (Udahemuka 2009). Therefore there is a clear case for further exploration of the use of subsidy and targeted supplies of inputs as a means of social protection for resource-poor farmers (United Nations Food and Agricultural Organization 2008).

A new vision for agriculture in Africa

Major challenges facing farmers in SSA include erratic climatic conditions, low soil fertility, low crop yields, high post-harvest losses and difficulties in accessing credit and agro-inputs. The soil fertility problems can be attributed to the abandoning of traditional shifting cultivation and land rotation systems for continuous cultivation without soil fertility replenishment (Rockström 2003). This, however, is due to population increases, which render those systems no longer feasible, and lack of income to purchase fertilizers, as discussed above. Recent estimates suggest that 70 per cent of farming activity globally is undertaken by smallholder farmers working in resource-poor and rain-fed agriculture (ibid.), and further, that around two billion people in developing countries derive some or all of their livelihoods from farming (Hazell et al. 2007). It is certainly easy to argue that a growing global population with changing consumption habits might be fed only by large-scale industrial agriculture. However, it is being increasingly argued that, in terms of global food security, the view that smallholder agriculture is a backward and unproductive way of life that must be 'modernized' is to miss an opportunity. Certainly, with rising demand for food and increasing oil prices, significant attention is being redirected to the role of small-scale agriculture for the triple goals of reducing economic poverty, building stronger communities and working in balance with ecological systems (Wilkinson 2008).

The concepts of social and environmental/ecological resilience are increasingly important for making the link between the general well-being of the human population and the ever-changing ecological system. Resilience captures the idea that all livelihoods need to be able to adapt to complex and continual change (Rockström 2003;

King 2008). King (2008) argues that low-input and holistic agriculture systems such as some form of organic agriculture, bio-dynamics, community-supported agriculture, permaculture and community gardening are all attempts to evolve adaptive systems. It is an important aspect of such systems that they are not purely focused on farming in harmony with nature, but also equally value the creation of enhanced well-being in human societies. While such systems and philosophies have coalesced as a range of small-scale popular movements in western Europe, the United States, Japan and Australia, the concept of the ecologically and socially resilient livelihood applies equally to the broader sweep of small-scale agriculture (Pretty et al. 2003).

Seasonality is a fundamental challenge for small-scale and subsistence farmers. Their knowledge of the seasons, their choice of crop varieties, access to land and land husbandry practices are all important components of the extent to which they are able to sustain and build a livelihood. Rain-fed agriculture has always been a risky and precarious undertaking, and in order to mitigate the unpredictability of the seasons, and particularly the timing and quantity of rainfall, farmers have adopted a range of adaptive practices. For example, they may diversify the range of crops or non-farm income generation activities. However, pressures on farmers to adopt commercial crops and mono-cropping practices combined with the loss of indigenous knowledge may have left them even more vulnerable to seasonal changes (Rockström 2003).

It is also likely that human-induced climate change will exacerbate the vulnerability of these same farmers and so may increase their poverty. While predicting the exact pattern of climate change is difficult and fraught with uncertainty, it is agreed that the next decades will see an increase in vulnerability to extreme weather events such as meteorological drought and floods. Further, it is likely that the timings of monsoons and rainfall will become less predictable (United Nations Development Programme 2007). The Intergovernmental Panel on Climate Change prediction is that in many water-scarce regions, water availability will be reduced through increased evaporation and changes to run-off and rainfall patterns.

Vulnerable livelihoods that are dependent on rain-fed agriculture can be devastated by a lack of resilience in coping with seasonal access to water. Resilience as defined by the Resilience Alliance is the ability of integrated systems of people and nature to adapt to change and to absorb shocks and stresses to the system. The success of rain-fed agriculture is crucially dependent on the knowledge and resources of farmers in coping with the unpredictability of rainfall. Seasonality has always been part of agriculture. Larger farmers try to manage this by constructing dams and choosing varieties of crops to suit their location; therefore investment in appropriate agricultural infrastructure is vital.

Research shows that the poorest households are dependent on rain-fed agriculture. In drought years, production can be non-existent and households may have to depend on food aid. However, some argue that we must distinguish between agricultural drought and meteorological drought. Meteorological drought is defined as occurring when the amount of rainfall falls below the minimum required to produce a functional harvest of food, whereas agricultural drought is the poor availability and uptake of water by the plants themselves. Rockström (2003) argues that meteorological drought is much rarer than we believe, but when it does occur, farmers will require social protection. Agricultural drought can occur when farmers, through lack of knowledge, resources or support, are unable to implement measures to ensure their increased resilience to the seasonality and unpredictability of rainfall. A particular example here is in the collection, storage and usage of rainfall (ibid.). More resilient farmers can diversify income sources, grow a wider range of crops, change their land use practices or add non-farm enterprises to their activities. In SSA, economic growth rates tend to be closely tied to rain, and this reflects the fact that a large proportion of such economies is dependent on the agricultural sector (United Nations Development Programme 2007).

Predictions for the future are dire: the 2007/08 *Human Development Report* predicts that in northern Sudan temperatures will rise by 1.5°C between 2030 and 2060 while rainfall will drop by 5 per cent, giving a 70 per cent decline in production of sorghum. However, 2030 is still relatively far away and rain-fed agriculture is still the backbone of food supply for the majority of the world's poor. Much can be done now to increase the resilience of livelihoods, but the focus in agricultural policy needs to be on how to support resource-poor farmers in coping with the increasing unpredictability of the seasons.

While agriculture has been ignored in development policy for the last decade in favour of the good governance and MDG agenda, significant attention is now turning back to the crucial role of local food production rather than export-led commercial production. It is argued that investment in the sector will improve the productivity of staple food crops that are consumed and traded locally by the poor and, thus, can stimulate local economic development (Department for International Development 2004). Agricultural activities are a foundation in building a sustainable livelihood for most families in SSA, as is shown by research in Tanzania, and therefore supporting and improving small-scale agriculture offers potential gains in well-being (Toner 2008).

On the other hand, commercial farming requires consolidation of small lands. This has proved to be socially and economically disruptive owing to appropriation of common lands and the taking back of land previously rented to smallholders. Small-scale farmers consequently become wage labourers and/or migrate to non-farm enterprises, resulting in depeasantization and reduction in production of local commodities (Bryceson 2000). Although large farms may be preferred for their low transaction costs in accessing goods and services (Hazell et al. 2007), they are not necessarily more productive and efficient. Pretty et al. (2003) have shown that low-input and environmentally sensitive agriculture can demonstrate significant productivity gains for small farmers. Moreover, the extensive use of machinery, clearing of vegetation and continuous mono-cropping associated with large farms tend to reduce soil fertility and increase pest problems, which necessitates the extensive application of inorganic chemicals, leading to pollution, destruction of biodiversity and high production costs.

Irz et al. (2001) argue that supporting small-scale agriculture will lead to increased farmer incomes, on-farm and non-farm employment, better nutrition and health, reduced food prices, social capital development, generation of local tax revenues and demand for better infrastructure.

The degree and form of these linkages are likely to be affected by factors such as the amount of rural infrastructure, rural population density, the need for immediate and local processing of farm produce and the nature of technical change in farming, and the tradability of both farm output and the goods and services demanded by farming communities. (Ibid.: 454)

Small-scale agriculture plays a significant role in supplying food. Nagayets (2005) estimates that Malawian small-scale farmers' contribution is 85 per cent of total agricultural production and that Ethiopian dairy smallholders contribute 97 per cent of national milk production. Production of food at the local levels minimizes food miles, reducing fossil fuel consumption and distribution costs, and thereby reducing food prices and making food affordable for low-income food-insecure households.

There is also a need to consider the role of agriculture and gardening in the city environment as a key component of sustainable development. The role of urban agriculture in contributing to global food supply is starting to be recognized, given the need identified above to localize food production in light of the possible reduction in reliance on fossil fuels.

Cuba is the one country in the world that has already attempted a transition in agriculture from large-scale fossil-fuel-based production to low-input, environmentally sensitive production, and it holds many lessons for African agriculture. The background to the transition was a sudden crisis in accessing food, oil and agricultural inputs following the collapse of the Soviet Union. The Cuban government's favourable agricultural policies, reform and support for small-scale agriculture during the 1990s in the midst of the United States' economic embargo on Cuba helped the country to combat its looming food crisis. Conversion of state farms to small farms and use of indigenous farming technologies and new biopesticides and biofuels propelled Cuba from food shortage to food sufficiency (Rosset and Bourque 2005). The transition was achieved through small farms and backyard production. Similarly, use of vacant plots and backyards in the cities for food and animal production increased fresh produce availability throughout urban centres at lower than farmers' market prices and ensured food security in Cuban families. The result was improved health and better performance in the World Bank Development Indicator rating in 2001 (Murphy 1999).

Cubans became involved in food production in Havana through the state-supported infrastructure for urban agriculture. In 2005, it was estimated that Cuba produced 4.1 million tonnes of urban-area harvest of vegetables, herbs and spices, in urban farms, intensive gardens, plots of land and family gardens, employing 354,000 people. These efforts led to improved food security, and urban agriculture has played a significant role in achieving food security and food production through Cuba's firm commitment to the idea, despite tough economic and environmental conditions (Rosset and Bourque 2005). Cuba is not alone in seeing the potential of agriculture in urban areas. Initiatives from the United Kingdom to Malawi to Argentina see this as a force for reconnecting people with nature and growing nutritious food close to people's homes in a way that encourages social cooperation. When described in this way, the intersection of environment, society and economy is obvious (Mkwambisi 2009).

While the *Human Development Report 2007/2008* contains a gloomy prediction that the developing world will become more dependent on the rich world for food exports, this may not be true. It cites the case of Malawi as proof of how drought undermines coping cycles and undermines the resilience and sustainability of livelihoods. Yet the reasons for severe declines in food security in Malawi were not all drought related, but rather related to the lack of support given to the Malawian agricultural sector. For example, in Malawi a 15–22 per cent increase in maize production was achieved during 2006, resulting from subsidy to small farmers, and the increase has continued (Future Agricultures 2008). While it may be argued that subsidy creates dependency, the programmes in Malawi prove that there can be a short-term productivity gain. However, in the longer term investment in research, water harvesting and marketing will be required. The *Human Development Report* talks about social resilience in terms of safety nets, but fails to provide an adequate consideration of ecological/environmental resilience.

Therefore, policy should focus on measures to increase the resilience of small-scale farmers in coping with seasonality and unpredictability. This may be through appropriate rainwater harvesting and distribution and better access to inputs of seeds, fertilizers and knowledge of how to increase productivity. However, there is a wider challenge that will require greater support for the development of strong national and regional food markets in Africa. Farmers will need to be supported to diversify their activities and to develop appropriate collective institutions. Attention should also be paid to linked processing activities that add value to agricultural products, creating stronger employment opportunities in off-farm activities and therefore decreasing the vulnerability of rural livelihoods.

Greater understanding is required of how farmers adapt to climate change, but also how farming systems can be made more resilient to fluctuations in rainfall. It is likely that the knowledge and technology already exist, but that the political will required to transform rain-fed agriculture is still lacking

Conclusion

This chapter began from a starting point that recognized the significance not only of agricultural activity in African economies but also as a sector that plays a significant or dominant role in the lives of most Africans. Hopes that a natural evolution towards an industrialized and 'modern' future as farms commercialized and peasants left the lands have not been fulfilled, nor did the neo-liberal era and structural adjustment lead to a great transformation. We have charted how an understanding of agricultural livelihoods in Africa must be based on an appreciation of both colonial and post-colonial attempts to distribute, settle and control land-based production. The aftershocks are still visible in the vulnerability of African populations that rely on the land for their livelihoods. When production fails, the state or external actors must step in or starvation awaits. Resilient and sustainable agriculture is the key to food security in Africa, but how this is achieved remains controversial. It will require an equitable and effective distribution of land and access to agricultural inputs and extension services. Such investment both by governments and external actors has been lacking in the last thirty years. However, a new set of rights may also be required, as conceptualized by the food sovereignty movement, encompassing rights to the means of food production.

We have to accept that seasonality and unpredictability are inherent features of humanity's relationship with the natural world. However, if we are serious about tackling rural poverty and the food insecurity that characterizes chronic poverty, then rain-fed agriculture requires urgent attention. Simply wishing away such agriculture by pointing to future hopes of modernization is to ignore the evidence of the last fifty years. So-called modern agriculture is itself looking vulnerable to declining fertility from intensive production and from the challenges of climate change. A new form of agriculture that is both ecologically and socially resilient is a challenge for us all.

FOUR

Big men and little women: the politics of gender in Africa

> More countries have understood that women's equality is a prerequisite for development. (Kofi Annan, seventh secretary-general of the United Nations, 2001)

It would be presumptuous to assume that is it possible to generalize about gender in Africa, as the process of becoming, and the experience of being, male or female, man or woman, varies across the continent. Being an 'African woman' or an 'African man' cannot be reduced to a set of characteristics. However, it is possible to trace a political discourse of gender. It is very clear that women on the continent are statistically poorer and less educated; more often victims of sexual violence and HIV infection; and restricted in terms of ownership of land and other productive assets. This chapter focuses mainly on the position of women, but also on the broader theme of inequality. We acknowledge that in understanding gender, it is necessary to also consider issues of men and masculinity. They are the other side of the same coin, and it is often the structural manifestations of patriarchal societies which trap women in poverty and ignorance. However, neither should we pretend that gendered identities are necessarily pre-eminent or all-encompassing or the only line of cleavage in relation to structural inequalities. We might equally explore disability, for example. Gender also interacts with other aspects of identity – religion, nationality, ethnicity – and some aspects of these have been explored in other chapters. Further, both age and wealth also shape the gendered identity and experience. A girl born into a wealthy family in a capital city will have a very different life experience from one born to a poor family in a remote rural area. Young people of both genders may find their voices unheard in family and political arenas, since the views of elders hold greater value and respect, and it is disrespectful for the young to challenge them. Ideas of how to be a proper 'man' or a proper 'woman' in society will certainly shape the activities, actions and possibilities of individuals of both genders.

In this chapter we discuss a number of themes that frame the politics of gender relations in Africa. First, the history of gender as a construct and theme in the discourse of state and nation, and specifically the adoption of formal 'rights' for women as defined by international conventions and agreements. This includes comment on their adoption and application within Africa. Second, the chapter goes on to analyse the construction of women's livelihoods, issues of access to education and political representation for women. In all sections we are keen to compare an often positive rhetorical commitment to gender equality with lived realities and structural inequality. This uncomfortably also sets the scene for the following chapter on the politics of health in Africa, in which gender inequalities, contextualized by poverty, lead to 'ideal' conditions for the HIV/AIDS pandemic to take root and spread.

In many African countries, it is clear that constitutionally, and in political rhetoric, the equal rights of men and women are well recognized. This chapter opens with an overview of international agreements on gender and approaches to women's development by external agencies and women's movements, which have all contributed to the shaping of African political discourse on gender, as have multiple and diverse ethnic conceptions of gender, and the more monolithic 'modernizing' influences of colonialism and missionary religion.

Women's livelihoods in Africa are still largely tied to the reproductive space of the home, working the land or within the informal economy, yet their ownership of land and access to credit often restricts their ability to expand and develop. The benefits of educating women are proven both in terms of economic output and in controlling fertility. However, in many countries women's access to education remains restricted, partial and of poor quality and relevance. Nevertheless, in many countries girls are now schooled in comparable proportions to their male counterparts. An increase in the political presence of women on the continent is also visible in some countries. However, this is still exceptional, and many women in political office also come from the more wealthy and influential families. Women and girls account for 60 per cent of the HIV-infected population in Africa, and they also bear the heavy burden of caring for the sick and orphans which the disease has created. Recent research suggests that HIV prevalence relates directly to national measures of gender equity.

Many of the arguments on the vulnerable position of African women are not new and are covered comprehensively in a broad literature and in the campaigns of active women's movements across the continent. We do not wish to offer a picture of misery without hope for all the women of Africa, and we should also look more positively at the continent. Sub-Saharan Africa performs far better on many measures of gender empowerment than does South Asia or North Africa. While we do not deny that there are significant areas of structural inequality between men and women on the continent, these are not as institutionalized through religion and politics as in other parts of the world. Instead, in this chapter and the one that follows we argue that it is the vulnerability of productive livelihoods and lack of access to decent basic services, rather than the structural inequality of genders, which is most significant.

The international discourse of gender

Since 1945 the United Nations (UN) has, in general, addressed itself to people's civil and legal rights and those of specific groups (United Nations 1996). The UN has also energized the global women's movement by proclaiming the 1975 International Women's Year and organizing the first conference on women, in Mexico, to assess the situation, highlighting strategies and goals for women's advancement. The conference plan of action – 'Equality, development and peace' – reflected the broad interests of Northern, Southern and Eastern Bloc women. It also focused on women's access to education, employment, political participation, healthcare services, housing, nutrition and family planning. The years between 1975 and 1985 were designated the Decade for Women. In 1981, the UN Convention on the Elimination of All Forms of Discrimination against Women (CEDAW) was adopted. The Convention was implemented in 1979 and by 2010 had been ratified by 185 countries (including 51 of the 53 African countries – the exceptions being Sudan and Somalia). CEDAW provides international standards for protecting and promoting women's political, social, economic, legal and cultural rights. It established a woman's right to vote, hold public office, be employed and establish contractual relations to reproduce by choice and to determine the nationality of her children. Progress in global gender equality is slow because, among all human rights instruments negotiated under the auspices of the UN, CEDAW has provoked the highest expressed reservations among governments (ibid.: 72).

CEDAW articles acknowledge that social and economic norms that deny women equal rights with men also render women more vulnerable to physical, sexual and mental abuse. Although CEDAW has been ratified by the majority of African countries, a number of countries, including Senegal and Tanzania, have been very slow to fully implement the legal changes required, owing often to cultural and religious misgivings (Ijeoma and Nkiru 2008). Systemic and structural barriers remain very real obstacles to the realization of women's human rights, though reformed and effective legal systems are able to challenge such barriers in some individual cases. For example, Ijeoma and Nkiru (ibid.) cite a case in Tanzania upholding the right of a widow to inherit land in the face of customary inheritance through the male line.

UN proposals for the advancement of women were restated at the 1993 Vienna Conference on Human Rights. The UN and governments were urged to ensure the full participation of women 'as both agents and beneficiaries of development', in addition to affording them 'the full and equal enjoyment' of human rights (United Nations 1996: 60). Women's rights and gender equality in development have, since the UN Women's Decade (1975–85), been emphasized by the 1994 Cairo Conference on Population and Development, the 1992 Copenhagen World Summit for Social Development and the 1995 Fourth World Conference on Women in Beijing. The implementation of CEDAW principles requires regular reporting of sex-disaggregated data on many indicators. Progress is monitored using the UN Gender-related Development Index and Gender Empowerment Measure (GEM).

The June 2000 UN General Assembly New York Conference on Women 2000: Gender, Equality, Development and Peace in the 21st Century assessed the progress and readopted areas of concern from the Nairobi and Beijing platforms: poverty, environment, conflict migration and empowerment. Highlighted as areas of focus were the role of men and boys in achieving gender equality and demands for greater access to HIV/AIDS treatment by women and girls.

UN General Assembly conferences have an atmosphere of pomp

and circumstance that forces attending government officials and delegates to sign empty commitments. The damning proof is that after several official recommitments in 2000, the UN Commission on the Status of Women's 2005 report on the progress of the Beijing platform revealed that there had been little progress in twelve critical areas, including poverty and economic empowerment, human rights, health and violence. These conclusions formed the background theme to the annual March 8th International Women's Day, in 2005: 'The role of women in wealth creation at the household level'.

Development agencies support educational reforms because of the influence they have on family size and health, as well as children's learning. Children of literate mothers are more likely to attend school. Thus, while women's contribution to agriculture is not in doubt, their exclusion from rights to property such as land, limited access to loan schemes and limited education mean they are generally unable to access knowledge of improved agricultural methods. Yet when female farmers do have access to microcredit schemes (which do not charge high interest rates) or have some education and access to agricultural inputs, not only do they raise yields, but the well-being of the family improves because they invest in better nutrition, education and health. Education fights poverty by empowering women in many other areas. Even in countries with universal primary education, there is a need for gender-aware affirmative action policies to improve enrolment, retention and quality of education for girls. Educating women helps to make societies and communities healthier, wealthier and humane (Gizelis 2009).

The African Union (AU) is committed to not only achieving but exceeding the targets set by the Millennium Development Goals (MDGs), according to a review of the African Union Commission (African Union 2005). The AU is further committed to the principle of gender equality and equity. It was formed on a 50/50 gender parity basis. One in every five national members of its parliament is a woman, including its first speaker. In 2004 the Protocol to the African Charter on Human and People's Rights of Women in Africa was adopted by heads of states and seventeen countries signed it. The New Partnership for Africa's Development (NEPAD) is expected to enhance women's human rights through the social development indicators included in its African leaders' Peer Review Mechanism.

Since 2000 the Millennium Development Goals have shaped UN discourse in relation to gender. Goals three and five, specifically, target gender equality:

Goal 3: Promote Gender Equality and Empower Women
Goal 5: Improve Maternal Health

The substance of Goal 3 is premised in targets that seek to achieve not only equality of access to education, but also access to waged employment and political representation. The *Millenium Development Goals Report* (United Nations 2008) shows that some progress has been made in sub-Saharan Africa (SSA), with 89 girls in primary school for every 100 boys (rising from 83 in 1990). In 2005, 80 girls were attending secondary school for every 100 boys in SSA (but this is a small decline from 82 in 2000). This figure also disguises the fact that access to secondary school is highly constrained for both genders across the continent. Lloyd and Hewett (2009) argue that the picture across Africa is very diverse, with many countries having already achieved gender parity in education enrolment at the primary level, but with others, such as Niger, lagging behind. They also argue that completion rather than enrolment is a better measure of impact, and Africa has the lowest levels of primary school completion in the world, with great underlying diversity. Eight per cent of girls and 19 per cent of boys in Niger complete primary school in comparison with 90 per cent of girls and 86 per cent of boys completing in South Africa. Significantly, in a number of countries (including Tanzania and Zambia), the completion rates for boys have fallen. In relation to employment, 31 per cent of women in SSA are in waged (non-agricultural) employment (as compared to 25 per cent in 1990). However, studies show that a significant majority of such jobs are insecure and low paid.

Political representation of women has increased from 7.2 per cent in 1990 to 17.3 per cent in 2008, with Rwanda leading the world (ahead of Sweden) with 48.8 per cent of political representatives being female. Such gains have been achieved largely by quota systems, and later in this chapter we will discuss the politics of representation. So, the picture in SSA in relation to these measures is generally positive. It is likely that the continent as a whole will soon reach gender parity in access to and completion of primary school, and a number of pioneers led the way in the formal political representation of women. Shifting persistent structural inequalities takes generations, but perhaps such changes offer the possibility of a different future in relation to gender.

However, the picture for health, and in particular maternal mortality, is less positive. Maternal mortality in SSA has declined from 920 per 100,000 live births in 1990 to 900 in 2006, and the UN admits that progress on this goal is 'negligible'. Access to skilled medical assistance remains low in SSA (47 per cent of births in 2005 from 42 per cent in 1990), while progress is also slow in reducing adolescent pregnancies (118 per 1,000 women in 2005, from 130 in 1990) and in decreasing an unmet need for contraception (24 per cent in 2005, from 26 per cent in 1990). Clearly 2015 targets are unlikely to be reached (United Nations 2008).

While international agreements do direct some attention to issues of gender, the lack of progress in achieving the MDG targets suggests some deeper structural problems. Chant (2007) argues that the MDGs are inherently weak on robust measures on gender equality and that they do little to reorient the neoliberal orthodoxy that values women as 'instruments' rather than 'agents' of development. It is, therefore, to the issue of women's role in both the productive and the reproductive spheres that we now turn.

Development discourses and women's livelihoods

It has long been asserted that women's livelihoods are undervalued and unrecognized in African development discourse and policy, and that in many contexts modernization, economic development and increasing religious fundamentalism (all supported by foreign aid in various forms) have in fact extended and entrenched the subordination of women (Berber and White 1999; Nnaemeka and Ezeilo 2005).

Boserup's (1970) research and assertive conclusions that modernization had marginalized women have inspired considerable scholarship that exposed male domination (Elson 1991) and the fallacy of gender-neutral development to a recognition of the differential role of Women in Development (WID) (Buvinic et al. 1978; Staudt 1985; Tinker 1990). Planners were criticized for ignoring and undermining women by privileging male views on women's activities and thereby overlooking considerations of time budgeting, local knowledge and the acceptability of projects to proposed beneficiaries. Earlier intensive, large-scale and infrastructural interventions had unintentionally harmed and sidelined women. The emphases on human capital, basic needs and technological development overlooked women's need for appropriate technology that they could afford and operate (Dauber and Cain 1981; Stamp 1989). They also failed to address the pressing development issues that are viewed as having most relevance to women – for example, women's health, education and employment. WID demanded separate projects to enable women to develop their human capital and to meet their basic needs.

Boserup had reported that the African farmer was not the 'he' of the official development policies, but a woman doing most of the agricultural work. She and others have argued that the work of African women (who constitute 60–80 per cent of agricultural workers) had been undercounted and undervalued in official demographic and economic statistics. Women's work was a valuable resource, but wastefully rendered 'invisible' (Bay and Hafkin 1976; Denton 2002) by the twin forces of capitalism and colonialism. In Chapter 3 we considered the nature of rural livelihoods in Africa, which remain predominantly reliant on small-scale agriculture, and discussed how the burden of labour in such systems tends to fall most heavily on women. Boserup (and many others) further argued that the introduction of cash crops increased work burdens on food producers. Women worked and men, in their role as *de jure* household heads, appropriated the cash. More recent research shows that economic development in terms of increased cash income to a household tends to translate into improvements in family welfare when women have access to and control over cash income. Gehab et al. (2008), in a study of childhood malnutrition in fishing communities on Lake Victoria, examines how women identify children as their first spending priority, but they are not mentioned at all as a concern by most men. This is also noted in recent work on social protection in Africa, which shows better outcomes for family well-being when cash transfers are directed to women rather than men (Barrientos and De Jong 2006).

When women migrate to cities to escape the restrictive rural economic opportunities and the restrictive conventions of family life, their lack of schooling often qualifies them only for low-paid jobs and self-employment in the informal economy. Urban dwellers depend on women in their various capacities as food growers, traders, processors, hawkers, servants, domestic labour and municipal public workers. This is supported by the 2008 MDG report (United Nations 2008), which suggests that, in SSA, 80 per cent of women who are employed work in low-paid and low-skilled positions. However, recent research suggests that it is more educated women and women who have more individual autonomy who are able to migrate in the first place, with the majority remaining embedded in the patterns, practice and vulnerability of rural life (Gubhaju and De Jong 2009).

As previously discussed, agreements on human rights and increased women's rights under the law have not easily matched women's ability to exercise them in order to take more control of their livelihoods. This has continued to deny many women the incentive of improving and applying skills and knowledge (Rogers 1981), and has led to measures to integrate women into all areas of development interventions by according them rights to inheritance, children and control over property. However, international actions since then have not necessarily strengthened the relative position of all women, but those with the resources and individual agency to act have been offered new opportunities.

WID proposed 'another development with women' using organizational collective action in order to achieve the economic and political empowerment of women (Development Alternatives with Women for a New Era 1985).

In the 1970s and 1980s development agencies incorporated WID in human capital development policies to provide training opportunities through either adding women-related components to existing projects or creating women's projects. Women's projects created additional unpaid work for women and, ironically, jobs for men. Women continued to do their domestic productive and reproductive work in addition to income-generating activities such as horticulture, animal husbandry, craft-making and cooperative labour at grain mills. However, because women lacked education and technical and marketing know-how, it was men who became empowered with marketing and managerial skills as they became project middlemen and salaried employees. Research demonstrates how frequently men came to occupy key positions within women's groups. This has implications for control over resources in relation to economic development, and also in terms of the representation of women where this is measured by the number of 'women's' groups. Helen Hambly Odame (2002) notes this in her research in western Kenya, as do Boesten et al. (2011) in their study of community-based workers in Tanzania.

WID research and interventions in Africa have successfully served as an antidote to gender-neutral policies and assumptions that men's and women's needs and responses to opportunities are identical. However, WID efforts to provide women with opportunities to participate in male-defined, male-dominated social and economic structures produced minimal changes in the conditions and situations of women. The prevailing cultural norms that privileged men with preferential treatment at the expense of women were an obstacle to changes promoted by WID. Objections to 'women's development exceptionalism' became common and are still manifested in constant reminders that women's human rights should not be achieved at 'the expense of antagonising men' (Cleaver 2003; Nyerere 1984; Ugandan AIDS Commission 2000).

When women-only projects are successful, families are fed and clothed, children are schooled and husbands' social and business ventures supported. In some cases husbands abandon all economic responsibilities to women, but whether women's projects are successful or not, they can invoke male jealousy and a backlash blamed for increasing violence against women (Obbo 2003; Momsen 2001). A number of authors also point to a crisis of masculinity caused by increasing opportunities for women in modern economies, which, it is suggested, undermines their previous position as economic providers (Cleaver 2003; Chant 2007). It is also argued that this increases domestic and sexual violence as men seek to prove their masculinity in the sexual rather than the productive sphere (Epstein 2007).

As WID had became synonymous with 'women only', a more holistic and reconciliatory approach, Gender and Development (GAD), came into use. GAD advocated the study and understanding of masculinities as a starting point for involving men in the development process. However, critics argued that this would undermine the struggle to achieve gender equality (Cornwall and White 2000). Tackling the problem of women's exclusion from development in Africa required an analysis of the process of exclusion. This is an area that we will return to in Chapter 6, with specific emphasis on HIV/AIDS and reproductive rights.

Gender and Development became a new paradigm, advocating a holistic assessment of the needs and strategies of both women and men when planning and evaluating the success of development. GAD development interventions call for a fundamental reassessment of gender relations and ideology (Marchand and Parpart 1995; Cleaver 2003). Advocates assert that economic improvement is impossible without political empowerment and suggest policy solutions to the intractable unintended results of development, such as the 'feminization of poverty' particularly associated with female-headed households (FHH).

Chant (2007) argues that the consensus view is that FHH are disproportionately concentrated among low-income groups and tend to suffer extremes of poverty compared to their male-headed counterparts. FHH are often thought to be the result of the predominance of men in rural–urban migration, male desertion, divorces and wars. Chant (ibid.) cautions that some FHH may exist through choice and are a result of the increasing agency of women. She also cites research that suggests that children brought up in such households may actually be better off in terms of nutrition, education and health. This can be seen as linked to control over assets (cash and non-cash), which women will tend to direct towards children (Gehab et al. 2008), as previously alluded to. Chant (2007) also argues that to some extent there has been a 'feminization' of labour through increased female wage employment, which exacerbates declining employment for men at the lower end of the societal hierarchy and increases women's responsibilities and male resentment.

A GAD approach focuses on the 'condition' and 'situation' of women in the development process. The condition of women is defined by their legal and economic statuses, which determine their access to health, education, technology and credit. The position of women pertains to the power-driven social relations between men and women (Young et al. 1981; Rathgeber 1995: 206). Thus, informed policies on gender cannot ignore the multiple power relationships in households and between social groups. GAD advocates the creation of a change-enabling environment through gender empowerment and mainstreaming. Empowerment entails the accessing and exercising of power by marginalized peoples. However, it is right to caution that overly individualized notions and expressions of women's rights may not be an appropriate and acceptable endpoint. Nzenza-Shand (2005) argues passionately for specifically African conceptions of women's empowerment, which would draw on the collective foundations of many African societies and would, for instance, accommodate polygamous marriage.

The 1986 UN World Survey on the Role of Women in the global economy and the 1989 update both recorded limited progress during the Decade for Women, and in Africa noted the negative impact of structural adjustment programmes (SAPs) on women. Under SAPs, women have borne increasing workloads and their unpaid labour has heavily subsidized cuts in social services and civil service retrenchment (Staudt 1985; World Bank 1989). Twenty years later, the 2009 version of the same report does not detail substantial progress for African women in this regard, arguing that the continuing neoliberal focus on cost recovery and privatization of basic services such as healthcare and water provision tend to disproportionately disadvantage women. Rightly, a new appetite for strengthening accessible and public provision of health and education in a number of African countries, such as Ghana, Tanzania and Malawi, is highlighted as a potential means of stemming this continual decline. The positive impacts of social protection mechanisms such as basic income grants and pensions in South Africa are clearly seen to have a beneficial impact on reducing household poverty, particularly for women and girls (United Nations 2009: 79). An increasing focus on social protection measures such as cash transfers combined with investment in basic services in primary education and healthcare has considerable potential to ease the dual burden of women as caregivers and producers.

Women, microfinance and entrepreneurship

One of the most popular and widely promulgated 'solutions' for the marginalized position of African women is microfinance and small enterprise. Among a plethora of donors and non-governmental organizations (NGOs), Dambisa Moyo (2009), while heavily critiquing government-to-government aid, also falls under the illusory spell of the promise of microfinance.

New stereotypes and simplifications are created in the process. The discourse that this has created tends to promote the constrained and latent agency of female entrepreneurship, which might be released by access to reliable sources of credit. NGOs and donor agencies often present case studies of the success stories – women who have started businesses and are now able to create better livelihoods and support their children to attend school.

However, microcredit is no silver bullet. The Grameen Bank model of group lending has not necessarily provided the assets required for sustainable businesses to thrive and to grow. Interest rates are excessively high and group lending creates social pressures that tend to exclude the poorest. Many such groups also do not inherently know how to run a business and receive little support (Rugimbana and Spring 2009).

Further claims are made for values-based business and livelihoods in transforming gender relations and livelihoods; for instance, Bassett (2010) argues that the production of Fairtrade Cotton in Mali and Burkina Faso brought in regulations that required female ownership of land. In reality, men used their wives to front businesses that they controlled.

Also, the organic agriculture championed in the previous chapter is claimed by the International Federation of Organic Agricultural Movements (IFOAM) to be more favourable to woman owing to lower use of harmful chemicals. However, it is said by others to potentially increase women's burden of work as methods are more labour intensive.

There are further barriers to women as entrepreneurs that impede the dream outlined above. Hampel-Milagrosa and Frickenstein (2008) argue that in southern Africa three times more women than men are working in the informal economy, as they face far greater barriers in formalizing and growing their businesses. Legal and customary restrictions on women entering financial agreements, especially with regard to land and property ownership, impede many women in attempting to enter into formal business arrangements. The colonial periods in many countries also marginalized women's political power and reconfigured gender relations, compared with the pre-colonial period. Further policy reforms that promote private ownership often reinforce and extend such inequality. In particular, Hampel-Milagrosa and Frickenstein argue that World Bank efforts to promote business expansion through increased credit tied to individual private asset ownership result in women largely becoming trapped in an ineffective and low-level microcredit cycle, as they are not able to access sufficient private assets.

Therefore it is clear that while broad-brush generalizations are possible concerning the livelihoods of women in Africa, we should be cautious of considering these in isolation, as to simply consider the oppositional relationship of man and woman is mistaken. The extended family may here be key as it is the most influential factor in shaping the formation and progress of enterprise in Africa (Smith 2009). Such a conclusion throws up a far wider and more complex set of relational processes, relating to trust, representation, voice and social capital in wider society.

The power to be heard: representation and voice

The preceding section highlights how the contribution of women to the economy, both productively and reproductively, is undervalued in Africa (as it continues to be globally). It is evident that efforts to increase women's economic development are often only marginally successful given the structural inequalities that exist between men and women, but also the positions those men and women occupy in wider society. It is key to the analysis of gender in Africa that, in terms of development outcomes, what matters alongside the overall poverty level of a household are the access and control that those members have over assets and resources. The same point can be made for any household within a society. In this section we examine processes of representation and voice in the political process in Africa, which are vital in understanding power and control over resources at both the micro level of the household and the macro level of the state.

In 1993, an internal World Bank evaluation of WID programmes (World Bank 1993) observed that most staff were convinced that if integrating women's concerns into programme delivery makes projects more economically efficient, then ultimately they will be included without special effort or manipulation (Rathgeber 1995: 210). However, this rather rationalist and utilitarian argument overlooks the fact that, routinely, donor agencies as 'brokers' of development and modernization have served the priorities of male-dominated host governments. Therefore, agencies' capacities to effect societal change in recipient countries are limited by the constraints of their governments' policies and their dependence on the cooperation of local officials. The sexual division of labour and the social relations of gender, with all the in-built power and economic inequalities, are 'reified as culture and placed out of the mandate of development' (Marchand and Parpart 1995: 228; Goetz 1991; Stamp 1989). Sovereign rights are sacred and social transformation is not a development issue (Young et al. 1981; Marchand and Parpart 1995: 235). This reasoning finds resonance in the attitudes of local male leaders who are offended by the suggestions of women's development (World Bank 1989), as is also demonstrated in the weak implementation of CEDAW in many African states. Development interventions that attempt to operate outside mainstream government positions are doomed to failure. GAD campaigns have sought to influence the agenda of institutions both in donor and recipient countries. In Africa, GAD advocates seized the historical 'moment' in the 1990s to push the agenda of 'mainstreaming' women after SAPs made politics and development openly intertwined. Donors were insisting upon political reform as a condition for receiving funding. Reforms included democratic elections and transparency and accountability in public actions. Donors promoted 'civil society' development to monitor the actions of states. A number of governments in SSA have also experimented with gender budgeting in relation to public services delivery, most notably South Africa.

In Africa, NGOs mushroomed to campaign for debt relief, women's political participation, women's property rights, human rights, and girls' education. The conditions seemed right for the GAD agenda to become a reality, with women's organizations pressuring for social and political change; the universities providing research support for policy planning in gender; parliamentary women working for legislative reform; and women lawyers defending the civil and human rights of women (Chant 2007). However, the proliferation of women's groups, rather than strengthening efforts at forging strong national feminist movements, may have undermined them. Elite women spoke for, and not with, the ordinary women, and often reflected the concerns of their class and ethnicity rather than gender (Nnaemeka and Ezeilo 2005; Chant 2007; Orock 2007). The exception to this might be South Africa, where women's role in the struggle meant that they played an important role in the African National Congress (ANC) (figures such as Winnie Mandela), and they were successful post-1994 in ensuring that the new South African constitution did not incorporate and formalize customary law (against opposition) that would have sanctioned the marginalization of women, although the realities of modern South Africa's poverty, HIV and inequality make the lived reality very different for most women (Waylen 2006).

Official measures of gender empowerment such as the UN Gender Empowerment Measure use data on the representation of women in parliament, ratios of male and female salaries and the proportion of women in professional, managerial and technical employment to attempt to quantify the level of 'agency' that women have within particular states. However, we need to be cautious about their use in SSA as the figures exclude the vast majority of women who work in the informal sector and, again, potentially only highlight the empowerment of elite women (Chant 2007). Many African nations are not able to provide the required data for inclusion in the GEM (United Nations Development Programme 2009). Of those that do, South Africa is ranked at 26 (of 109), Uganda at 49 and Ethiopia at 85. Many of the Arab states and South Asian countries perform far more poorly than SSA on this measure.

Constitutional affirmative action, including allocating parliamentary seats to women, has been adopted in a number of African parliaments, including Burkina Faso, Uganda, Tanzania, Malawi and South Africa. An increasing number of women are also successfully competing for parliamentary seats, and Rwanda has a total of 48.8 per cent of women in parliament (both as quota members of parliament, but also freely elected), leading the world on this particular ranking (ibid.). This might be explained, to some degree, as a consequence of the 1994 genocide, which left 30 per cent of households with a female head, and their subsequent role in the post-conflict reconstruction, but also on the current Rwandan government's view of women as the conduit of development. The outcome of this level of female representation (achieved largely through the reservation of seats for women) is yet to be fully analysed in terms of its wider impact on gender inequalities in Rwandan society (Matume 2004).

However, some accuse women parliamentarians of failing to articulate the interests of women and merely of looking pretty and doing nothing. Tamale (2000), writing about Uganda, and Geisler (2000), writing about South Africa, both argue that the incorporation of women into mainstream politics has in effect co-opted and constrained more radical women's movements and that women in parliament rarely have the institutional support to shift structural inequalities. The press, colleagues and electorates also tend to reinforce the message to women that their place is at home bearing children and cooking for their husbands. This is recognized by Morna (2007), who argues that an increasing voice for women in the media is required to combat negative stereotypes of women. It is argued by some that in fact women who make it to the top are not emancipated and lack the support of other women. Further, that women need to organize themselves, independently of the state, to increase their own self-reliance, to assert their independent right to make choices and to control resources that they need to eliminate their subordination (Keller and Mbwewe 1991). This line of thought assumes that grass-roots-based women's movements are needed to put more women in politics in order to achieve the critical mass that will make them an effective empowered voice and force for demanding governments' commitment to development, empowerment, human rights and political participation (Orock 2007). Many view the election of Ellen Johnson-Sirleaf in Liberia in 2006 as confirmation of progress in this area, considering her to be an intellectual, bureaucratic and activist president. However, her biography is typical of the elite in Africa, irrespective of her gender (Johnson-Sirleaf 2009). While the percentage of female politicians is relatively easy to ascertain, a tiny proportion of the population will attain such a role, and in weak states government and state services may have little direct impact on the everyday lives of the population.

In relation to the micro level, many see an answer to problems of political representation in community-led or community-based planning and management of resources. Such systems are often seen as being potentially beneficial and empowering to women. In reality, the benefits of participation in development activity often do not reach the poorest or address structural inequalities. Marginalized groups (including women) tend to be structurally excluded (by barriers of time, health, money) or self-excluded (through fear of speaking in public, perceived lack of education) (Cleaver 2005).

In addition, the local ownership that is often quoted as a means by which communities gain the power to shape and to use services

(World Bank 2002) can in practice lead to small groups of middle- to high-wealth individuals within communities increasing their own strategic and political agency through controlling resources. Furthermore, local management does not necessarily guarantee access by excluded groups. Their problems are accessing a service that is not necessarily recognized as valid by community decision-makers. This is supported by evidence from Tanzania (Sokile et al. 2003; Cleaver and Toner 2006).

There is growing evidence that current participatory mechanisms can often reaffirm existing social inequalities as participation requires the possession of a certain level of assets (be they social, human or financial), and the poorest may not possess the resources to enable them to participate at all (Mercer 2002), let alone sufficient political and strategic agency with which to challenge existing power structures. Differential opportunities for the participation of men and women have been a particular area of focus in this regard. Cornwall (2003) argues that efforts to promote participation can be shaped by 'gendered' interests, which often exclude women. As Cleaver (2005) also notes from her research in Tanzania and Zimbabwe, women may not feel able to speak out in public spaces and may not be represented in institutional arrangements. This has been widely recognized in efforts to create participatory spaces with women – in particular, being excluded by lack of political voice, cultural and religious ideas of proper behaviour and existing institutional structures (Cornwall 2003; Hickey and Mohan 2004; Wordofa 2004; Coles and Wallace 2005; Kabeer 2005).

Kabeer (2005) and Cornwall (2003) both note that efforts to create and increase the political or organizational participation of women at the local level have tended to favour the participation of 'elite' women who are no more likely to represent the interests of poor women just by the fact of their being female. Kabeer (2005: 17) analyses different quota systems for promoting women's political participation and argues that such attempts to redress imbalances in women's political participation are inadequate: 'Women's presence in the governance structures of society clearly carries the potential to change unjust practices, but if the women continue to be drawn from a narrow elite, if they have been invited rather than elected, and if they have no grassroots community to answer to, their presence will be only a token one.'

Capture of collective community processes by elite groups (whether founded on wealth, ethnicity or caste) is a significant criticism of efforts to promote collective community action as a means of driving local development. Elite groups position themselves to maintain control over authoritative and allocative resources entering the community (Mosse 2001; Platteau and Gaspart 2003; Platteau 2004). These dominant and influential actors are able to refashion external interventions in ways they deem appropriate. Cleaver (2005) argues that the chronically poorest are excluded from participation in collective life through the multiple dimensions of their poverty, such as ill health and lack of education. It is important to recognize that participation and the opportunity to exercise active agency in collective spaces will not be determined by a single factor, but will be the result of complex and interlocking individual and collective forces. Another group that are often unable to use their active agency in collective spaces are children and youth. Again, as with gender, local norms of appropriate behaviour for the young may result in them having little or no voice (Gosling and Cohen 2007).

The power of stereotypes

Ideals and stereotypes of male and female identity are important contributing factors to the nature and structure of gender relationships and therefore to expectations of behaviour of men and women, which can include how each gender can represent themselves in the public sphere, and also how they shape acceptable norms of behaviour in society. Dolan (2003) considers how norms of masculinity are exacerbated in conflict situations through a consideration of the use of rape in northern Uganda. Aid and development interventions may inadvertently reinforce these oppositions; for example, Denov (2006) discusses how post-conflict reconstruction can reinforce gender stereotypes, with women being seen not as combatants but simply as 'camp followers'. Hence they have not benefited from cash payments made to their male counterparts, although they may have had very similar experiences. Gizelis (2009) and Jacobson (2006) both further argue that women should play a greater and more institutionalized role in post-conflict reconstruction as a means of broadening debates and offering alternative conversations in society, although they rightly do not assume that women are automatically and necessarily peacemakers.

This reaffirms the gender and development perspective that ideals of men and masculinity must be addressed. This is not only for the sake of women, but also for those men who also find themselves marginalized by such ideals. For example, homosexual men and women in Africa find themselves in highly vulnerable positions. Homosexual relations are illegal across the continent (except in South Africa, but considerable discrimination remains) and in some countries there are currently attempts to strengthen the law yet further. For example, Uganda is attempting to introduce the death penalty for homosexual acts that result in the transmission of HIV/AIDS. While there is often a deeply held indigenous intolerance of homosexuality, this has been reinforced by the religious institutions that find fertile soil in Africa (Bujra 2003).

Conclusion

This chapter does not pretend to offer an all-encompassing analysis of gender in Africa, but provides an overview of some of the central debates and policy discourse over recent decades. It has highlighted the fact that women remain significantly marginalized in Africa both in terms of the capacity to construct sustainable and productive livelihoods in their access to adequate education and healthcare, and, as the next chapter will show, in their vulnerability to sexual and domestic violence. Yet we have noted that across the continent government commitment to gender equality is strong and that women's political representation in some countries outstrips that in the rest of the world. Significant progress has also been made on gender parity in access to primary school. However, as we have discussed, this has not yet led to a structural transformation for women as a whole, and perhaps this is because this is not about gender equality alone.

It is argued that the success of gender mainstreaming crucially depends on educating women and men to be committed to changing gender relations and the structures that maintain them. Women must get involved in the interpretation of cultural practices, since they play a big role in the socializing of children. It is argued that women whose consciousness has been raised in participatory debates on governance and development analysis processes will lose their current voicelessness and be ready to demand their human rights to education, health (including sexual and reproductive health) and political leadership.

However, the same could be said of men who are trapped by poverty. They may have more power in the domain of the household or within their immediate community, but it is likely that they are only a little more empowered or emancipated than their wives. The conclusions are not straightforward. In purely developmental terms, a society clearly benefits from having a population of educated and healthy women. Men and women will always exist in relation to each other and so any structural transformation that is likely to occur would need to be rooted in a change in the expectations of society on the roles played by men and women, but also in the structure of the extended family and wider society. That said, it is also essential that we look beyond narrow arguments on gender to a broader recognition that the growing inequality in Africa is not only gendered, but more fundamentally material in origin.

FIVE

More than HIV/AIDS: the politics of health in Africa

Our cemeteries are filled beyond capacity. Parents are dying from HIV/AIDS or burying their children; a generation of fathers and mothers is being lost leaving the grandparents to grieve and raising the next generation. I cannot overstate the terrible nature of the crisis that is enveloping our societies. As bad as it is today, the reality is that it is getting worse. (Speech by H. E. Girma W/Giorgis, president of the Federal Democratic Republic of Ethiopia, 2004, Commission on HIV/AIDS and Governance in Africa 2004)

Introduction

While it has been possible for some to argue that people in Africa are materially poor, but maybe more spiritually and socially fulfilled than the inhabitants of wealthier nations, this should not allow us to overlook the significant burden of ill health that characterizes the continent. Poor health is therefore not simply a description of the condition of the continent; it is perhaps the starkest indicator of political failure. Africa is the global epicentre of the HIV pandemic, where it is the highest cause of death in women of reproductive age. (Add to this the persistently high levels of maternal mortality discussed in the previous chapter.) Half of all global deaths from malaria occur in sub-Saharan Africa, with children aged under five and pregnant women particularly at risk, and tuberculosis continues to be a significant killer. Add to this water-borne infectious diseases and parasitic infections caused by poor sanitation and contaminated water, the impacts of unregulated environmental pollution in urban and some rural areas, high levels of death by road accidents and a general baseline of food insecurity and malnutrition, as outlined in Chapter 3. It is very hard to romanticize this list and it is by no means all-inclusive.

When a sub-Saharan African becomes ill or an accident befalls them, it is highly unlikely that an efficient health service infrastructure will be available. The levels of well-trained medical personnel cannot meet the heavy demands of the population, their numbers being too few as they enter training, but further depleted by HIV/AIDS and the lure of better-paid opportunities overseas. Health systems and infrastructure offer a patchy and inadequate mix of state and private provision (including NGOs and religious institutions), with many essential drugs in short supply, but ironically others also too easily available in an unregulated market. Yet most people (the cash-poor farmers) are unable to purchase drugs or access treatment. While government ministers fly off to London, Switzerland or Dubai for treatment, the poorest must simply wait for death at home or turn to alternative forms of treatment.

Significant evidence links ill health and chronic poverty. If you are sick, you cannot work or attend school, and the family resources must stretch to meet your needs. If you require hospital treatment then the family may have to sell productive assets to fund your care, the immediate need being greater than the long-term accumulation. Therefore health is fundamentally a political question; it is a key signifier (more so than economic growth) of the state of a nation and of the provision of basic services, as it is also inextricably linked to education, water and sanitation and food security.

Health in Africa is about much more than HIV/AIDS, although it can be hard to see beyond this given the significance and dominance of the issue in recent decades. However, in this chapter we offer a socio-political analysis of the HIV/AIDS pandemic in Africa, but this should be read with the caveat that many of the issues discussed are also relevant to the broader burden of ill health and inadequate health infrastructure. This exploration enables us to interrogate a number of foundational issues in understanding contemporary politics in Africa, including the role of the international aid industry in shaping discourse and action and the interface of 'traditions', 'myths' and 'modernities' in relation to health

HIV/AIDS – the politics of poverty, sex and aid

In Africa today, increasing numbers of people are living with the HIV/AIDS epidemic in ways that are changing the very character of everyday life. Many societies are struggling to cope with the effects of this terrible disease, often in conditions of extreme poverty, conflict, weak institutional and physical infrastructure, and deficient educational and healthcare systems. A true process of immiseration can be observed in many parts of the continent, particularly eastern and southern Africa. Here, the epidemic is creating a downward spiral whereby existing social, economic and human deprivation is producing a particularly fertile environment for the spread of the virus. In turn, the virus is also compounding and intensifying the deprivation already experienced by people (Poku 2006).

Despite a generation of intense research, Human Immunodeficiency Virus (HIV), the cause of Acquired Immunodeficiency Syndrome (AIDS), remains resistant to any of the present chemotherapeutic controls. In 2008, there were estimated to be 22.4 million people living with HIV/AIDS in sub-Saharan Africa (SSA), two-thirds of the global total. While the rate of new infections has decreased since a peak in 1996, the numbers of people infected are still increasing: 14.1 million children in SSA are estimated to have lost one or both parents to the disease. Access to antiretroviral (ARV) therapy, which slows the advance of the disease, has increased substantially owing to targeted aid funding. However, it is estimated that for every two people globally who can now access ARVs, five new people will become infected (United Nations 2010).

The first observation to make is that HIV/AIDS is both a crisis and an endemic condition. It is a crisis because the speed of spread of HIV has proved quite awesome. In some communities, infection rates have increased from 2 per cent to 25 per cent in adult populations in less than four years. Thus, before people are even aware that infected families and friends surround them, their communities have been deeply penetrated (Poku 2006). That endemic condition may best be simply illustrated by the fact that in an already affected country, even if there were to be no further cases of infection, the pain and trauma of the deaths of those already infected will continue for the next generation and the social and economic repercussions of their deaths will continue for generations to come.

The second observation is that the epidemic manifests itself not only as a specific problem, but also a pervasive one. Its specificity is revealed in its associated morbidity and mortality. There are increasing numbers of people, mostly healthy productive young women and men, getting sick and dying. The response in the first three decades of the epidemic addressed this quality of the crisis. It focused on the epidemic as a health crisis and consequences for health service delivery. However, in the regions most affected, the repercussions of these deaths are beginning to permeate and affect every facet of human life and national development.

Though not always explicit, the presentation of hyper-sexualized societies in Africa as an explanation for the rapidity of spread of HIV/AIDS on the continent has been largely accepted, perhaps because it taps into a much deeper Western social consciousness. As we noted in Chapter 1, in much of the Western popular imagery the African continent has long been associated with all that is instinctive, primitive and sexual. In truth, there is little proof to support this, and to date no evidence exists that shows that people from Botswana, Namibia, South Africa, Swaziland or any part of Africa are more sexually active than people from France, the United Kingdom, Germany, the United States or Japan. Moreover, the scientific world dismisses the notion that males from any continent, or indeed region, are more addicted to sex than those from another, because testosterone levels, the measure of sexual vigour in men, never vary more than a tiny fraction of a percentage anywhere in the world. What is in contention here is not that particular social patterns (including sexual behaviour) are exposing Africans to a greater risk of contracting the HIV virus (a point to which we shall return), but that there is something in the culture of Africa or in the sexual mores of its population that easily explains their plight. Clearly, sexual behaviour is an important factor in the transmission of sexually transmitted diseases. It alone, however, cannot explain why HIV prevalence is as high as 35 per cent of the adult population in some African countries and less than 1 per cent in the developed world.

Discomfiting stereotypes about 'African' sexual mores and behaviour have long coloured HIV prevention discourse, a tendency pointed out a decade ago already by Green (1994). These stereotypes flatten the diversity of African societal realities, social systems and cultural patterns into an imaginary 'African culture' and harbour subtexts not dissimilar to assumptions and pronouncements popularized during the heyday of colonialism. This tendency has been most evident when explanations have revolved around notions of 'African culture' and 'traditions', with these putative 'characteristics' frequently assigned to entire regions and even the continent at large. One early and startling effort, for example, tried to associate different sexual and reproductive strategies with specific racial groups (ibid.). More sophisticated efforts have subsequently focused on the ideological or cultural dimensions of the epidemics (Rushton and Bogaert 1989), often laying emphasis on the need to change societal norms in order to reduce the spread of the virus. Such perspectives tend to neglect the deadly interplay through-out history between infectious disease, social relations and material conditions (Caldwell et al. 1989), AIDS being a recent case in point, and such vantage points tend also to pass over the fact that 'culture' is heterogeneous, is socially and historically constructed and does not adhere 'naturally' to any place or group. Thus, one finds epidemics in southern Africa often attributed to a paradoxical confluence of sexual promiscuity and public bashfulness about sex, with these 'character-istics' commonly attributed to 'African culture' or 'African traditions'. However, the evidence shows that, at least until the early colonial era, most societies in the sub-region were marked by high degrees of sexual education and regulation (Kark 1949). Those ideological frameworks and social arrangements, however, were mutated or 'morphed' by the cumulative impact of missionary Christianity, colonial conquest and societies' coerced incorporation into capitalist patterns of accumu-lation that centred on the extraction of primary commodities (prin-cipally diamonds, gold, copper and coal in southern Africa). The combination of proselytizing missionary Christianity (and its strategic positioning as a gateway to education and health opportunities for the colonized), and the intensive and coercive social engineering that was used to ensure reliable and cheap supplies of migrant labour, helped reshape the ideological and social arrangements defining societies and recast the ways in which sex operated in the public domain (Delius and Walker 2002; Coovadia et al. 2009). Although, in some quarters, this line of reasoning may seem to encourage a romantic harking back to a pre-colonial 'golden age', it best serves as a reminder that culture is socially and historically constructed and evolves amid a lively interplay with changing material conditions and social relations. Emerging from such tumultuous dynamisms are sets of norms and values that define, among other things, gender relations that govern the sexual aspects of social life and continue to evolve (Chabal 2009).

Unfortunately, much HIV literature tends to skirt such frames of analysis and ends up detaching patterns of sexual behaviour and disease from the social relations and material conditions in which they are embedded and from the constantly evolving dynamics that generate those relations (Walker et al. 2004).

For example, the gendered contours of HIV risk are profound. Women and girls, in particular, encounter numerous HIV-related risk factors that stem not from individual choice, but are embedded in the social relations and material realities of their societies. In some countries, much of the very early sexual activity for women takes place within marriage, and such early marital sex carries a threat of HIV infection in areas where HIV prevalence is high and their male partners are substantially older (Kamali et al. 2003). In many cases, such 'age mixing' is tied to the prestige of families that bond for mutual benefit, or to economies of need and aspiration. However, the older men are also more likely to have been exposed to HIV, all the more so in countries with high background prevalence. In Kisumu, Kenya, among women three years or less younger than their husbands, none was found to be infected with HIV, but half the women ten years or more younger than their husbands were HIV positive, while a study in rural Uganda has found that, among HIV-infected women aged fifteen to nineteen, 88 per cent of the girls were married (Pisani 2003). Young women are biologically more susceptible to infection, their sexual relationships might be more long standing and stable (thus they may have sex more frequently with each of their partners) (Glynn et al. 2001) and their partners might include older men who are more likely to be infected with HIV. Epstein (2007) argues that such concurrent relationships involving overlapping but long-term relationships, such as in polygamous marriage, may contribute to the pattern of the virus in Africa.

In most of southern Africa and much of East and Central Africa, the web of HIV transmission is much more extensive than in West Africa, with casual and so-called transactional sex appearing to feature more prominently in the epidemics. Multiple partnerships, it seems, carry greater likelihood of infection for young women than for young men, even where young men report more such partnerships than do young women. Given the already very high HIV levels in the general populations of many countries in these sub-regions, the odds of a person encountering an infected sex partner are high. Combined with factors that additionally aid HIV transmission (such as other STIs or biological vulnerability, as in the case of girls whose less than fully mature genitalia increase the risk of contracting HIV), such high background prevalence hugely increases the chances of infection. Consequently, many women in the highest-prevalence sub-Saharan African countries are becoming infected almost as soon as they become sexually active, as data from Kenya, South Africa and Zambia have confirmed. In a study in Zambia, 18 per cent of women who said they had been virgins a year before being tested for HIV were found to be HIV positive, while in South Africa, 21 per cent of sexually active girls aged sixteen to eighteen tested HIV positive (Glynn et al. 2001). HIV infection levels among young men spike considerably later, typically after the men reach their mid-twenties.

A good deal of evidence is available to buttress the general consensus that male circumcision protects against HIV infection. Even when controlling for other variables (such as sexual behaviour patterns), cross-sectional studies have concluded that male circumcision reduces the risk of HIV infection from female sexual partners by more than twofold (Buvé et al. 2002). A couple of complicating details must, however, be noted. First, circumcision does not eliminate the risk of HIV infection, it only reduces it (Weiss et al. 2000). Second, circumcision appears to protect only when performed before puberty and before the person becomes sexually active.

Leaving aside the role of physiological and biological factors, in rough epidemiological outline, the scale and intensity of a heterosexual HIV epidemic depends largely on

1 the extent of high-risk behaviour practised by men (principally the buying of sex);
2 whether and to what extent women have sex with men who display high-risk behaviour;
3 the extent to which those women, in turn, are linked into sexual networks with other people who also have unprotected sex with multiple partners.

Where the latter behavioural patterns are widespread, sexually transmitted HIV epidemics are more likely to become and remain rampant. Conversely, where most of the women who have sex with 'high-risk' men do not also have unsafe sex with other people or do so very rarely, those behavioural patterns tend to inhibit the scale of a mainly heterosexual epidemic. Men infected during paid sex infect other sex workers, as well as their wives, girlfriends and other sex partners, who, in turn, may transmit the virus to their babies. The perimeter of this web of transmission is therefore fairly restricted and the scale of an epidemic of this sort will depend largely on the proportion of men who have unprotected paid sex (Gray et al. 2000). Currently, many of the epidemics in West Africa appear to fit such a description and appear to lack the structural and 'environmental' dynamics that have propelled the much more rapid and widespread HIV transmission in southern Africa, for example (Pisani 2003).

Patterns of sexual behaviour are embedded in complex and often opaque social relations, which in different respects and to differing degrees may favour or hinder viral transmission. In this sense, there-fore, the various epidemics in SSA also express particular configura-tions of social, cultural and economic orders and occur on various templates of social relations. Indeed, it seems impossible to divorce the epidemics, particularly in southern Africa, from the socio-economic (including gender) inequalities, the widespread poverty and the bur-geoning cultures of consumerism that mark parts of that sub-region. In the high-prevalence parts of SSA, sustained inroads against the epidemics in all likelihood will remain inadequate as long as these social templates continue to be reproduced.

Sociocultural and economic factors

There is general agreement that population mobility, especially migration, can be a key factor in HIV epidemics. This is especially evident in southern Africa, where the largely seasonal or temporary character of migration, with migrants returning home to their families on a regular basis, most probably facilitated the rapid spread of HIV. In South Africa, for example, HIV prevalence has been found to be twice as high among migrant workers (26 per cent) compared with non-migrant workers.

The overall patterns of mobility in southern and parts of East Africa emerged from the engineering, since the late nineteenth cen-tury, of labour regimes designed to facilitate specific patterns of capital accumulation. These were centred largely on mining as well as agribusiness, later also encompassing urban manufacturing and service economies. Transport networks were explicitly developed to service these economies, with major rail and road systems linking harbours, mining hubs and agricultural basins. The resultant patterns of circular migration split (mainly male) workers from their families and communities for long periods of time (Lurie et al. 2003). Especially in southern Africa and parts of East Africa, these migrant labour systems distorted and dislocated family and community structures, radically recast social relations and aggravated women's economic dependence on male partners. The patterns of migration established were circular, with workers returning home at regular intervals, before travelling back to cities and towns for a further stint of work. Even during the apartheid era, these patterns were transnational (with the South African economy, for example, using migrant labour from Lesotho, Malawi, Mozambique, Swaziland and Zimbabwe).

The arrival of HIV in the sub-region coincided with dramatic changes that affected population mobility and systems of migrant labour. The gradual demise of apartheid since the late 1980s had already enabled more cross-border migration. This increased exponentially in the 1990s as formal and informal regional trading ballooned. Inside South Africa, internal migration also increased substantially as the enforcement of apartheid laws crumbled. Throughout the sub-region, women in particular became more mobile, their migratory quests for work often stemming from increasingly insecure livelihoods in rural areas.

Large-scale migration in the context of impoverishment, deep socio-economic inequalities and social dislocation appears to provide an ideal terrain for the spread of STIs, a combination of factors that has been in stark evidence throughout the sub-region (Crush and Frayne 2010). Conditions favour HIV transmission, for example, when men are separated from families and customary frameworks of social regulation, have some disposable income, lack many recreational options and live or socialize in low-income communities marked by strong gender and other inequalities. Workers such as (seasonal) plantation labourers, truckers, military personnel and mineworkers seem especially vulnerable to HIV. Very high infection levels have been reported in areas beside major transport routes, at border crossings, near military bases and around mines and agricultural estates. Social constructions of gender and sexuality also boost HIV vulnerability, not least among migrant labourers, many of whom work and live in hazardous, insecure and estranging surroundings that often encourage exaggerated bravado and risk-taking, including with sex (Kark 1949). The same pattern can also be observed in conflict and post-conflict settings.

Such wrenching forms of social engineering, carried to extreme heights in apartheid South Africa, arguably left shallower imprints in much of West Africa, where women were able to develop greater economic autonomy via their prominence in market trading and other forms of commercial activity. The overlapping impact of gender and socio-economic inequalities appears to be especially harsh in southern Africa, where meagre income-earning opportunities exist for women with little or no education, leaving them highly reliant on remittances from male partners and other kin. Indeed, at least one recent study suggests that women remaining behind in rural hinterlands sometimes engage in sexual networking as part of their survival strategies. The study, carried out in Hlabisi (in South Africa's KwaZulu-Natal province), found that among HIV-discordant couples, 20 per cent of women were HIV positive while their migrant husbands were HIV negative. This suggests that the women had engaged in sexual networking that did not involve their husbands. Anecdotal accounts from southern Mozambique point in a similar direction (International Organization for Migration 2003).

In addition, over the past two decades industrial sectors in which female workers predominated (such as garment manufacturing) have been hard hit by job losses after the withdrawal of subsidies and lifting of tariffs. This has further weakened women's economic status, aggravating gender inequalities and exacerbating women's risk situations. Research in Mamdeni, South Africa, for example, has persuasively correlated exceptionally high HIV infection levels, widespread transactional sex and job losses in the female-intensive textile and garment industry after the removal of tariffs and subsidies (Lurie et al. 2003). The same industries in Zimbabwe and Zambia have also suffered severe job losses, which have further impoverished women and, plausibly, acted as accelerating factors in the HIV/AIDS epidemic's evolution. The dynamism of income inequality in relation to HIV in SSA would seem to occur largely between men and women in the bottom two or three income quintiles, especially in settings that are socially and spatially highly stratified.

Transactional sex, therefore, would seldom link women in the bottom quintile with men in the top quintile. Instead, such relationships would tend to express material inequalities in the lower income rungs. In most cases, transactional sex appears to slot into the survival and aspirational strategies of women, particularly impoverished women. The United Nations Secretary-General's Task Force on Women, Girls and HIV/AIDS in Southern Africa has concluded that transactional sex and age mixing have become the norm in many countries in the sub-region (United Nations Secretary-General's Task Force on Women, Girls and HIV/AIDS in Southern Africa 2004). Transactional sex therefore simultaneously reflects men's generally superior economic position and access to resources. Men aged in their late twenties and thirties, however, are more likely to be HIV infected, and the dependencies built into such relationships severely curtail women's abilities to protect themselves from HIV infection (Gregson et al. 2002).

As noted, the most common explanations of transactional sex with older men hinge on assumptions of economic desperation. Particularly in urban areas, these relationships are formed amid aggressively propagated cultures of consumerism and in the midst of extreme juxtapositions of abundance and deprivation. As a result, sexuality, survival and consumption have become closely intertwined. Prevention strategies aimed at reducing unsafe sex have to be built on recognition of the fact that, for many women, sex can be one of the few valorized forms of capital at their disposal (Delius and Walker 2002).

At the same time, it is important to recognize the variety of other reasons why people have sex, irrespective of their material conditions. Besides the obvious importance of procreation and the overlooked role of hormones, sex is involved also in people's need to have fun, to seek and express trust, to build status and self-esteem, to escape loneliness, or to relieve boredom (Stephenson and Cowan 2003). Research in South Africa, for example, indicates that in the context of deep impoverishment and high unemployment (and the absence of affordable recreation), sexual relationships often feature in bids to boost self-esteem and peer status, or simply relieve boredom and torpor (Human Sciences Research Council 2008). What makes these quests particularly dangerous for so many women is that they are played out not only in areas where HIV has firm footholds, but in circumstances marked by glaring gender and other inequalities.

In this battle, the enemy is cunning and the armoury is sparse

For nearly three decades it has been the position of many observers of this grotesquely pervasive epidemic that politics, not medicine, has been its dominant feature. Consequently, it is in the political arena that a solution has to be couched, as much as it has to be searched for in medical terms. Yet productive responses on the part of political leaders, particularly in the most affected countries, had not been forthcoming until very recently. Denial or obfuscation were the orders of the day, but the epidemic's pervasiveness and finality has at last impelled some serious attention (Kalichman 2009). At the global level, growing awareness of the huge funding gap faced by developing countries has translated into political rhetoric to scale up international commitments, the most prominent of which was the setting up of the Global Fund to Fight AIDS, Tuberculosis and Malaria (GFATM) to provide a high-political-profile institutional framework for mobilizing resource in donor countries.

Global mechanisms (that were similarly focused on addressing one set of issues such as HIV/AIDS) were also set up by donors in the form of the United States' President's Emergency Plan for AIDS Relief (PEPFAR) or the World Bank's Multi-country HIV/AIDS Program (MAP). Meanwhile, developing countries' governments and private foundations such as the Gates Foundation also raised their contributions. In total, it is estimated that the available resources for tackling HIV/AIDS increased from US$1.1 billion in 1999 to $9.1 billion in 2008 – see Table 5.1 (Jewkes et al. 2001). This period saw a rapid increase in bilateral donor commitments from $240 million in 2000 to $4.8 billion in 2008, mainly because of PEPFAR. Multilateral commitments also rose rapidly from $300 million to $2.4 billion, largely on account of the Global Fund. Among United Nations (UN) agencies, the World Bank represents the largest source of AIDS funding, with cumulated commitments of $2.5 billion during the 1990–2006 period. Through its Multi-country HIV/AIDS Programme, the World Bank has approved $1.1 billion in multi-year grants or interest-free loans to support AIDS programmes in developing countries, particularly in Africa.

TABLE 5.1 AIDS commitments by source, 1999–2008 (US$ billion)

	1999	2000	2001	2002	2006	2008
Bilateral donors and European Community[1]	240	700	753	976	1,250	4,735
World Bank[2]	205	210	341	273	479	281
Global Fund[3]				332	830	856
Foundations/NGOs[4]	87	150	200	200	200	250
Domestic spending (local governments and households)[4]	500	500	500	1,000	2,000	2,000
TOTAL	1,032	1,560	1,794	2,781	4,759	8,122

Notes: 1. Data for 2000–08 are from DAC database (OECD) adjusted by subtracting research expenditures and contributions to Global Fund. For other years, data were obtained from government budgets and Kaiser Family Foundation publications. 2. World Bank database. Includes HIV projects and the HIV components of health projects. 3. Global Fund database. 4 Data from UNAIDS publications on the cost of the AIDS response.

There is very little evidence that the cause, intensity and direction of the epidemic have been seriously affected by prevention efforts that have, since the 1980s, relied on the same recipe in various combinations and with differing emphases, but has got us to where we are now. The global spread of the HIV/AIDS epidemic, as shown in Figure 5.1, does not show anything that could by any stretch of the imagination be described as success in prevention. In fact, we might want to stop calling this thing an 'epidemic' – an event with a foreseeable end – and instead admit that it is now an 'endemic' – a presence with which we will all have to live (and die) for as far as we can see ahead. Neither can we claim to have a good strategy ready for the future. There is no vaccine and an effective vaccine is still ten to fifteen years away, if it is possible at all. While antiretroviral medicines have fallen in price and are becoming more widely available through the GFATM, PEPFAR, the Gates Foundation and the Clinton Foundation, it remains difficult to make them affordable and universally available. Importantly, they remain complex and difficult to provide to all who need them in poor countries, and second-generation treatment to combat the onset of viral resistance remains beyond the means of developing countries.

In her book *The Wisdom of Whores* (2008), Elizabeth Pisani suggests that the HIV disaster is at least in part the result of an ideological

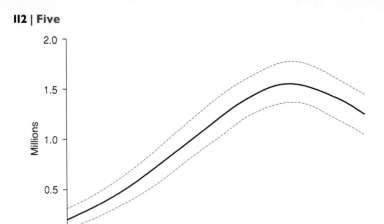

(a) Annual AIDS-related deaths in sub-Saharan Africa, 1990–2009

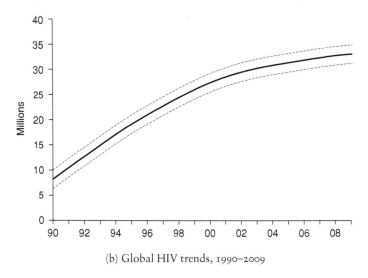

(b) Global HIV trends, 1990–2009

FIGURE 5.1 Number of annual AIDS-related deaths in Africa (*source*: UNAIDS, Global Report on AIDS Epidemic 2010, 2010, p. 22)

obsession among the agencies in the 1990s that 'HIV is a development problem'. In other words, that the issues to be addressed were poverty, education and women's rights, rather than the simpler base cause, sex. Pisani is wrong about HIV not being a development problem; it is (see Table 5.2). However, Pisani is correct to draw attention to the power of ideological obsession that has distorted the institutional response

TABLE 5.2 Close and distant determinants of HIV infection and possible prevention responses

Determinants	DISTAL →	MIDDLE LEVEL	PROXIMAL
Determinants	Macro-environment Wealth distribution Income distribution Culture Religion Governance	Micro-environment Mobility Urbanization Access to healthcare Levels of violence Women's rights and status	Biology Virus sub-types Stage of infection Presence of other STIs Gender Circumcision of men Behaviour Rate of partner change Prevalence of concurrent partners Sexual mixing patterns Sexual practices and condom use Breast feeding
Interventions	Redistributive social policy Legal reform and protection of human rights Taxation and fiscal reform Debt relief Reduction of corruption Adjustment of terms of trade with resulting effects on producer prices and wages International agreements on provision of low-price ARVs	Legal protection of women's property rights Legal protection of women and children Social protection of women and children Regulation of wages and working conditions	Syndromic management of STIs Blood safety Behaviour change via information, education and communication Condoms, male and female, promotion and marketing Female-controlled chemical barrier methods – microbicides VCT IVDU harm reduction Antiretroviral therapy during pregnancy Antiretroviral therapy as treatment for AIDS

to the epidemic. What were these obsessions? The first and simplest to engage with is the obsessive promotion of the ABC – Abstinence, Behaviour change and Condoms – approach. The second is the transfer of prevention strategies and ideas focused on condom promotion derived from the gay epidemic in the United States to a very different set of environments in the developing world, particularly Africa. The third is the way that the epidemic has been used as a vehicle for mobilizing resources for other significant concerns, notably poverty alleviation and threats to global security, and it should be said very clearly here that, on close examination, these turn out to have little to do with HIV/AIDS, at least not in the straightforward way that many in the advocacy industry would claim.

Over the past two decades, many of the institutions charged with the governance of HIV prevention programmes have prioritized ABC as the only way forward, particularly in the developing world. The problem with the ABC approach, however, is that the neat alphabetic label confuses the outcomes of successful HIV programmes with the message needed to achieve effective results. It also ignores the strong possibility that each of these components may be more or less effective or relevant depending on cultural, political and economic circumstances and the stage of the epidemic, early or late. Abstinence, fidelity or condom use are the successful outcomes of any behaviour-change strategy for HIV/AIDS. We have known this since HIV was identified as a sexually transmitted infection, and these are proven goals for all STI prevention. However, what is less well understood is how to bring about A, B and C.

The experience of Uganda is instructive. In its earliest responses, the government encouraged people to talk about HIV and AIDS and the result was a diversity of response. Of course, all who engage with the challenge of HIV/AIDS wish there were a 'magic bullet', a simple solution, that could get people to change their behaviour, but sexual behaviour is precisely not simple. It is not even about what people may most immediately think of as 'sex'. It is tied up in complex ways with people's diverse life situations, with property, kinship alliance, ritual and religious beliefs, ancestors and gender relations, income and inequality, land and livelihoods. Getting people to change their sex lives, therefore, requires addressing their realities. The best way to do this is to encourage those who fund and design prevention programmes to understand these diverse situations and to tailor messages to specific local needs, 'local' here meaning both geographically and socially local. Pushing for one overarching 'best' message will never be effective (Poku et al. 2007; Poku 2006). Uganda was remarkable in the extent to which it achieved diversity in prevention messages, but this was done by establishing a political environment that encouraged many actors with many messages (Epstein 2005; Stoneburner and Low-Beer 2004).

In contrast, the explosive nature of the African epidemics shows that, despite the resources devoted to condom distribution over the last twenty-eight years, there have never been sufficient condoms and people have been very reluctant to use them. As the death in April 2009 of Cardinal Alfonso López Trujillo, head of the Pontifical Council for the Family, reminds us, internationally and in some countries, Vatican opposition has been a factor. UNAIDS estimates that 13 billion condoms per year are needed to help halt the spread of HIV and other sexually transmitted infections. Yet the reality falls far short of this need. Resistance to condom use and reluctance to talk publicly about HIV/AIDS are not confined to the Catholic Church, but are also contentious issues in many of the fundamentalist Christian missions, which are a thriving business across Africa.

This socio-political analysis of HIV/AIDS can by no means cover all the nuances, consequences and causes of the last thirty years; and it underlines the complexity and enormity of the challenge in tackling the disease. Yet the politics of health in Africa is such that a focus on single diseases (while not underplaying their significance) is misguided. The slow response of African governments to the HIV/AIDS crisis is symptomatic of the condition of the African state in general and has already been discussed at length in this book. It is not surprising, then, that it is the aid industry which has driven and shaped much of the African response. Ironically, Epstein (2007) suggests that this global industry actually undermined indigenous and successful efforts in Uganda to reduce transmission rates. There is no doubt that, for some, the HIV/AIDS industry is a lucrative one, and whole livelihoods have been constructed and shaped around it. Research from Tanzania illustrates this evolution and offers the striking conclusion that, while large funds are available, they are having little impact on strengthening health systems, but have produced a fragmented patchwork of disconnected projects (Boesten 2009; Beckmann and Bujra 2010).

HIV/AIDS most starkly reveals the impact of poverty and powerlessness on the shaping of an epidemic. As noted by Poku (2006) and Chabal (2009), it has become a disease of the poor. Indeed, this reminds us that we also need to broaden our gaze from a narrow focus on HIV/AIDS, for the greatest cause of all communicable disease is poverty (Chabal 2009). Therefore, the remainder of this chapter attempts to offer a wider view on the politics of health systems in Africa.

Health systems – inadequate and failing

Millennium Development Goal (MDG) 6 seeks to reduce the biggest single killers in Africa (HIV/AIDS, malaria and tuberculosis). More than 767,000 people died from malaria in SSA in 2008, but the recurrent and endemic nature of the disease also creates a considerable burden on the productivity of an economy and of a family. Malaria has recently become the focus of high-profile aid campaigns, and new initiatives aim to supply treated mosquito nets to targeted groups such as pregnant women. Progress on malaria prevention is relatively easily achieved and the UN MDG report (United Nations 2010) shows a strong correlation between inputs of funds and access to treated bed nets and improved malaria treatment. However, it estimates that funds fall well short of the $6 billion required for full coverage, and there are growing disparities between rich and poor in the use of bed nets and treatment.

The argument for the focus and investment on single diseases (as in MDG 6) is justified in relation to the swift input of funds in order to achieve results. However, without the investment and creation of robust and comprehensive public health systems, such gains last only as long as the external funds continue to be present. As this book has already made clear, the state in most African countries has not been able to create such public services. As alluded to above, aid for single diseases runs the risk of undermining the creation of holistic public systems as resources flow to one specific issue and hence can divert the limited capacity of health systems where they exist. Research from Tanzania suggests that large inflows of aid have done little to improve public health systems in terms of responding to the HIV/AIDS crisis, but have created a cornucopia of fragmented, ineffective and opportunistic interventions, originating from affected communities and external organizations alike (Boesten 2009). It is argued that there has been little interaction between disease-specific programmes and health system strengthening that would improve the capacity to deal with all health problems, including the 'big three'. For instance, greater attention to infection control and the creation of safe health facilities could provide more specificity to efforts to strengthen health systems (Harries et al. 2010). Such programmes would need to reach beyond the meagre public health systems to those provided by religious institutions and NGOs, as in many countries they provide the greater part of the accessible care, although often on a fee-paying basis.

Even in the continent's richest country, South Africa, there are considerable challenges to the health system. Coovadia et al. (2009) suggest that although there is a reasonable health infrastructure in place, the system is challenged by insufficient investment in primary care and human resources. They also argue that systems are unable to adequately respond to the social determinants of health and disease and the very large inequalities between population groups in the country. As the previous analysis of HIV/AIDS in this chapter shows, the social and economic basis of transmission and vulnerability is fundamental to the way that the disease is spread.

Other MDGs in the list of eight which relate directly to health are those on which least progress has been made in SSA, and further underline the need for a more holistic and systematic approach to the politics of health.

MDG 4 is to Reduce Child Mortality by two-thirds by 2015. This has almost been achieved in North Africa; however, progress in SSA is slow, with a fall from 184 deaths per 1,000 live births to 144 in the period from 1990 to 2008 (United Nations 2010). Four diseases account for 43 per cent of deaths (pneumonia, diarrhoea, malaria and AIDS). The first three of these are preventable with relatively low-cost medications or mosquito nets, and we have already considered at length the complexity of vulnerability to the fourth. Vulnerability to infectious disease is also increased by the food insecurity and malnutrition that continue to be a pervasive feature of life for those reliant on subsistence agriculture, as the majority of people on the continent are. Low-cost prevention methods are available, but not always accessible.

For example, GFATM funding has enabled an increase in vaccination rates (SSA saw an increase from 55 to 72 per cent in immunization rates for measles between 2000 and 2008); however, such gains may not be sustained without health infrastructures to support them in the future. In many countries there is also fear and suspicion of mass vaccination arising from side effects and poor communication between public health institutions and parents (Streefland 2001).

MDG 5 is constructed around the aim to improve maternal health. As discussed in Chapter 4, decreases in maternal mortality have been hard to find in SSA. Most deaths result from haemorrhage, which can be prevented with skilled birth assistance and medical training – and again inadequate health systems vastly increase this risk. There are also many young mothers in SSA for the reasons already discussed above, and the most immediate problem for many girls and young women is not the risk of HIV/AIDS, but the higher risk of pregnancy, yet both might be prevented in the same ways. Girls with no education are four times more likely to become young mothers, and only 23 per cent of women have access to family planning (United Nations 2010). While official development assistance for health doubled between 2000 and 2008, the total amount devoted to reproductive health and family planning remains at the same level as in 2000.

The fundamental challenge for health systems in Africa is to provide comprehensive, holistic and accessible primary healthcare. This was well recognized in a relatively recent World Health Organization report on health and inequality (World Health Organization 2008). Issues of critical importance are the presence of skilled personnel, mechanisms of access for those who cannot pay, and access to equipment and medications. Each of these has proved problematic. Skilled personnel are too small in number to meet demand and are often lured away to the global North by better working conditions and rewards. User fees and corruption within health systems fundamentally limit access to existing facilities, and shortages of essential drugs and equipment remain frequent. Private and non-governmental facilities have not filled this gap in any consistent way and have certainly exacerbated inequality of access to care.

Chabal (2009) notes that what he characterizes as the 'informalization' of the state in Africa increases the powerlessness of the poor and has resulted in weakened state institutions. This, combined with recent international influence on the role of the market and cost sharing in the delivery of services, has fundamentally prevented the development of robust and effective primary healthcare systems.

Africa also carries a heavy burden of violence and conflict, which adds to the collective burden of physical and mental distress. Very recent history has seen large conflict events such as the Rwandan genocide, extended conflict in the Democratic Republic of Congo and the activities of the Lord's Resistance Army in Uganda, to name only a few, and to number all conflicts would require another book. However, poverty, marginalization and the breakdown of societies can result in a large number of dispossessed youth and a culture of brutality, and prescient examples might be found in the extremely high levels of violent crime in South Africa or among quasi-religious and ethnicity-based groups (such as the *mungkiki*) in Kenya. Chabal (ibid.) argues persuasively that colonialism and the evolution of the post-colonial state have eroded the communal foundations of existence. While social relations have been ruptured, modernity has failed to provide an adequate unifying moral framework and now faces a competitive moral fight from evangelizing religions and essentialized models of ethnicity. Conflict and violence therefore emerge from a political manipulation of difference.

It is also vitally important to understand that illness in Africa is a social and collective phenomenon. Parents, relatives and kin are all involved in obligations of care, causation and treatment. Given the absences of health systems and the nature of those that do exist, treatment is rarely free and family and kin are the first line of defence and the necessary collective pooling of resources, both material and non-material. It is this burden which makes a disease such as HIV/AIDS particularly destructive in that those who succumb are productive adults. Not only is their contribution to a family livelihood lost, but often their need for care places a huge burden on other family members, often grandparents and children.

There are also major psychological impacts associated with illness and accident in Africa, as they are often thought to have identifiable causes such as malevolent spirits or witchcraft. Such beliefs are very deeply rooted, and in times of crisis people will often turn to both 'modern' medicalized systems of treatment and to more 'traditional' forms of healing. It is possible to argue that the retreat of modern health systems also forces people (with few alternatives) to rely on traditional forms of healing and is leading to a 'retraditionalization' that is not necessarily favourable to healthier societies (ibid.).

Conclusion

This chapter brings together many of the themes that have been explored throughout this book. It considered the multiple and complex burden of ill health, accident and violence that the populations of African states bear. We used the HIV/AIDS pandemic to demonstrate the political, economic and social basis of disease and transmission, considering the increased vulnerability that comes from gender and material inequality. However, we have also used HIV/AIDS as a means to understand the manipulations and limitations of external aid interventions in Africa and highlight the political and moral dimensions of these interactions. We argue that a focus on single diseases is and continues to be an overly narrow and ineffective approach. In combination with the dysfunctional nature of the African state and external pressures to promote market solutions to social problems, little progress has been made on building comprehensive systems of primary healthcare. The provision of holistic primary care is intrinsically linked to poverty, vulnerability and inequality. It has a crucial role to play in reducing both maternal and infant mortality. Therefore, the right to health is a deeply political question. As we have noted here, the burden currently falls on families ill equipped to meet it, and ill health all too commonly pushes people farther into poverty. Suggestions that private providers or non-governmental providers alone can fill the gap are based on little global evidence, as the comprehensive health systems of northern Europe and China must attest.

Conclusion: an African renaissance

So fear not, my friend.
The darkness is gentler than you think.
Be grateful for the manifold dreams of creation, and the many ways
of the unnumbered peoples.

Ben Okri, 'To an English friend in Africa',
in *An African Elegy* (1992)

The African experience to date has produced a post-coloniality that indelibly imbues insecurity. There are palpable feelings of a job left undone, of failed dreams of modernity, of frustration at the incompletion of the nation-state project, of self-serving 'ethnicized' governing apparatuses and of an uncaring and xenophobic outside world that subjugates and alienates the majority of Africans from their rightful place at the table of human and social development. In short, there is a lack of pride, trust and confidence in that most visible of institutions of Africa, the post-colonial state. There are exceptions, of course, and it would be contentious to start naming any here. In retrospect, however, Fanon's notion of renovating violence, that real freedom for Africans could be won only by destruction, true liberation only through fire, has proved to be an ultimate perfidy. Violence in Africa has begotten more violence. The outcome is the culture of corruption, brutality, destitution and despair, some of the many facets of which we have addressed in the pages above. Yet the challenge for Africa remains immense. This book has explored the complexity and diversity of the continent and has sought to contextualize and problematize the issue of why and how African states have evolved in the ways they have. We have avoided unicausal explanations where possible and each chapter is intended to provide further interlinked analysis that emphasizes the relational and dialogical nature of politics, power, conflict and development in Africa. This final short chapter is, then, not intended as a definitive summing up, arriving at a neat conclusion to the multiple challenges.

Yet there is some value in restating several factors whose general incidences provide a theme on which the variations are constructed. The problem of stability and order – political and economic – remains a central one. There is a paradox here. In one sense, the state in Africa is immensely strong. It is monopolistic (Aron 1966). The state is the major source of employment, the major source of finance and the major partner in most economic enterprises; the existence of well-armed and numerous police, paramilitary forces and the army itself adds to that appearance of strength. Yet, in so many other senses, the state is weak. It cannot always provide the people with what have become thought of as the necessities of life, such as education, health facilities, a public transport network, employment and the affluence associated with vibrant development; that is an obvious sign of weakness. In many countries, the government cannot even implement its policies. It lacks the capacity to transform its rhetoric and policies into practical actions in the rural areas or among the underprivileged people of the sprawling urban centres. There is a gulf between the theoretical power of the state, as expressed in constitutions and statutes or proclamations, and the real power of the state as represented by effective field officers, widespread political support and economies growing in line with government expectations.

The trust that permits political actors reasonably to assume a set of self-restraining behaviour patterns by other actors has hardly anywhere been assured. The extractive and instrumental assumptions of players in the political arena are critical prerequisites for the unabashed readiness to use power to its full, which is such a predominant feature of the continent. Ibo proverbs graphically illustrate this point: 'I am against people reaping where they have sown,' a character in Nigerian author Chinua Achebe's novel *Things Fall Apart* (1958) says. 'But we have a saying that if you want to eat a toad you should look for a fat one.' Yet one must not 'take away more than the owner can ignore'. The moral of Achebe's story is that the restraints, which in other systems are provided by ideology or party loyalty, are absent and the result is the chronic instability and powerlessness so evident on the continent. The inequalities, which did not begin in the imperial years, but were extended, entrenched and reinforced, have become cumulative; the competition for scarce resources remains liable to be structured along ethnic lines; and the instrumental values of the polity reduce to a minimum that degree of party or national loyalty which enables unpopular measures to be accepted with a degree of equanimity.

So what is Africa's future? Dire predictions of the impact of climate change suggest that in the next fifty years Africa's problem with food security and dependency on food aid will reach new extremes. Continued levels of high population growth will continue to expand the population of young people on the continent. Young people, even while most will have some literacy, will not find formal employment and are disillusioned by a life on the land. They will be ever-expanding dispossessed mobs ready and primed for mobilization by the Big Men and Women who continue to live on the spoils of the state. With a lack of positive and progressive national identities, ethnic and religious fragmentation will continue to further fracture the continent. Intellectual and ideological alternatives are present and creative, but still weak, confined to the margins of public discourse, while pernicious forms of religious colonialism, both Christian and Islamic, exploit the desperation of many for a more hopeful future.

Governments, despite heavy inflows of aid, have failed to provide significant coverage of basic services and infrastructure; the recent decades of anti-state globalization have undermined the dream of the post-colonial paradise. Without a visible state providing some safety net, the family remains the site of security and dependency. With large extended families and high expectations of family responsibility, combined with high levels of inequality, then those who do succeed are often suffocated and compromised by familial demands.

It is fascinating that in the depths of the current recession no mainstream British political party has suggested that international aid should be cut. The United Kingdom Department for International Development now has a budget touching £8 billion per year. There have always been dissenting voices on aid, but they are gaining new strength and diversity.

Rwanda, a country heavily dependent on aid, has become a source of criticism both from Rwandan president Paul Kagame, who praises the 'no strings attached' infrastructure investments of the Chinese, and Paul Rusesabagina (of *Hotel Rwanda* fame), who lambasts Western governments (particularly the British) for continuing to pour in aid while turning a blind eye to the corrupt excesses and territorial ambitions of the Kagame government.

We certainly agree that it is time to question the mantra of 'more and better aid'. The UK Department for International Development spends increasing resources on cajoling a marginally interested British public to develop an 'understanding' of global development (under the banner of development awareness), but we are in danger of seeing only the 'emperor's new clothes'.

Two recent books have focused on the effectiveness of aid. Zambian economist Dambisa Moyo, in her book *Dead Aid* (2009), blames aid for the dependency and corruption of African states and sees salvation in capital markets and microfinance and NGOs. Yet her analysis does not really offer anything new. Such 'solutions' have been the battle cry for twenty years of neoliberal aid conditionalities.

Jonathan Glennie's *The Trouble with Aid* (2008) offers a more nuanced account, tracking both the positive and negative impacts of aid. He counts the positive direct impacts often aligned with MDG targets as the increase in numbers of children accessing school. However, he also charts the indirect impact of aid, such as the conditionalities that force poor economies to open up their markets, which has led to the destruction of local industries and reinforced dependence on the aid-givers. Glennie also questions the rhetoric of 'good governance', which has led to only marginal reductions in poverty, some disastrous privatizations benefiting mainly the elites and an excuse for governments to pass responsibilities conveniently to 'the people'.

Aid has become focused on policy reform, which does little more than produce extensive shopping lists and policy documents. Rather than encouraging governments to be accountable to citizens, it tends to vest power and accountability in the donors. It encourages reactive rather than proactive government. Aid fundamentally undermines the social contract between government and citizens, but as Glennie says, from the point of view of the donor, aid is easy and buys friends. That is much easier than really attempting to tackle the global inequalities and post-colonial history that have shaped and created Africa.

However, Glennie too has a blind spot (given his employment in international NGOs). He singles out government aid in his analysis and his conclusion points to a growing role for NGOs. However, they are equally as capable as government of creating dependency, supporting corruption and elite capture and imposing conditionalities, albeit on a smaller scale.

However, his general conclusion that Africa needs less and better aid is valid and he is right that, in tackling poverty in Africa, a far more serious and complex discussion is required concerning the role of trade, migration, climate change and taxation. All of these are major global transboundary challenges with no simple solutions. The power of the former colonial masters is itself waning and perhaps they rush to increase aid spending as they watch the influence of new players such as China and India extend their reach on the continent.

What is a more positive future? We have hinted at the long shadow of colonialism throughout this book and argue that there has been a colonialism of the mind and of expectation that has come to express itself as a defensive anti-identity framed by reaction against an ancient oppressor. We need an alternative vision and discourse for African politics that, unencumbered by the weight of policy 'doublethink', engages with the relationship between the state and family, changing forms of family formation, and the challenge of mobilizing and incorporating the youth in a new future.

At the heart of this must be the reinvigoration of an African intellectual tradition capable of theorizing the interface of multiple and diverse African cosmologies with a global narrative on rights, governance and democracy. Presidents Mbeki, Obasanjo and Wade, together with other African leaders, welcomed in the twenty-first century as the century of Africa, heralding an African 'renaissance'. The New Partnership for Africa's Development (NEPAD) and a rejuvenated African Union (AU) were supposed to reflect and direct this optimism. Yet the rhetoric so far has been little else but that articulated through vague aspirational targets associated with the equally vague and aspirational Millennium Development Goals. These have been accompanied by little in the way of achievable plans or properly funded projects that have the enthusiastic support of all stakeholders, including the much-elided and much-misunderstood mass of the population. The gross inequalities and lack of opportunities that perpetuate low morale, poor productivity, emigration and lack of association with, and pride in, national identity are still in place and continue to widen.

The answer, then, must lie within. While African communities, be they states, nations or ethnic groups, urban or rural, try to compare and contrast themselves with their peers elsewhere, particularly in the West, the result is likely to be a continuation of the current malaise and disillusionment. In order to do better, an individual must feel good about him- or herself. The same surely applies to political, cultural or economic communities. Given that the state is likely to be the most influential stakeholder among the other types of community mentioned, the need for positivity must start in that institution.

Nevertheless, while it is true that the state in Africa has certainly not been a helpful tool in economic or social development, it is also the most likely tool for motivating and catalysing such development in the future.

The barriers are all too clear – low skills, poor training, ephemeral tenancy of holders of influential policy-making posts, inappropriate selection criteria, inadequate funds from within (fiscal collection), external pressure on policy-making that is not often related to internal needs, to name but a few. The current barrage of 'capacity-building' components to development projects aimed at developing world governments do not help. This is partly because they are largely uncoordinated and have different, often competing, agendas. It is also because most are funded and, despite all the 'bottom-up' and 'grassroots' rhetoric, directed by Northern agencies and donor bodies that still aim to mould institutions in the image of themselves. Capacity-building is so often aimed at governments and policy-making bodies that donor and NGO bodies realize *have to be negotiated* in order to execute projects and programmes, not helping the situation. This is different from specific capacity-building in governance, which should become a main plank of activity, directed by the stakeholders in governance with help from those who have the experience and skills to train and teach, but whose aspirations, agendas and interests coincide with those of the most important stakeholder, the populations served by governance institutions, be they supranational (such as the AU), regional (such as the Economic Community of West African States, ECOWAS) and the Southern African Development Community (SADC), national or local.

In stressing this imperative, it is accepted that strong, effective and representative governance is key to social and economic development, from which human development is likely to ensue. However, in order to become proactive agencies of progress, institutions of governance have to be seen to be in possession of sovereignty and authority and able to make decisions on behalf of their constituents. The current climate of domination by external powers in policy- and decision-making will not relieve the increasing inequalities that are a root cause of dissatisfaction and low morale in contemporary Africa. This is not a recommendation for autocratic dictatorship. Neither does it say that liberal democracy, described here as a Western-centric ideology attached to the functioning of the capitalist world economy, is wholly inappropriate for Africa. Africans love voting when given the chance and when they believe there is something worth voting for.

A start to the process is the acceptance, both internally and externally, that much, though admittedly not all, of what is wrong with the post-colonial state in Africa is as a result of its inputs, both past and present. This, then, is the realization that the expectations, particularly of state governments in Africa, did not and have still not taken into account what was left behind at independence and what the inputs have been in the half-century or so since. These inputs include policy-making skills and experience in governance. Institutions of governance are not built overnight and cannot be created by politicians whose tenancy in their positions is likely to be short. In the European model, there is normally a permanent functioning civil service that actually processes the work of governance and advises politicians what is possible and what is not. This is where the experience and skills really lie. In Africa, even where a strong civil service exists, such as in Botswana and Senegal, such a body of experience is lacking and is prevented from forming by economic constraints, partly imposed from outside.

The second point that needs to be accepted is that Africa, particularly sub-Saharan Africa minus South Africa (which is fast becoming a new neocolonial force in its own right across the continent), and its people have never been given access to a level playing field in any arena. Politically, economically and socially, Africa and Africans have always had to fight against unfair barriers and pejorative and xenophobic treatment, not just from the usual white European and American culprits, but also from Africans who share a sense of otherness and lack of confidence in their own achievements and potential.

This is a condition of post-coloniality that exists as a mindset, a construct that encourages belief in the idea that Africans do not do things as well, quarrel unnecessarily, and are not as industrious as their Northern counterparts. The point of significance is that the erroneous perceptions described here are held not just by outsiders, but also by Africans themselves. This lack of confidence, imbued so indelibly during colonial times, has to be expunged with alacrity if Africa is to gain its rightful place on the geopolitical and socio-economic map of the world.

Bibliography

Achebe, C. (1958) *Things Fall Apart*, New York: Fawcett.

ActionAid (2002) *Farmgate: The developmental impact of agricultural subsidies*, London: ActionAid.

Africa Monitor (2009) *Development Support Monitor 2009: Africa in Our Hands*, Cape Town: Africa Monitor.

African Union (2005) *Audit Review of the African Union Commission*, Addis Ababa: African Union.

Agarwal, B. (2001) 'Land rights and gender', *International Encyclopaedia of Social and Behavioural Sciences*, pp. 8251–6.

Agricultural Research Institute (ARI) (2007) 'Making fertilizer subsidies work in Malawi', Briefing Note 0703, London: Africa Research Institute, December.

Ake, C. (1996) *The Marginalisation of Africa: Notes on Productive Confusion*, Malthouse Press.

Aron, R. (1966) *Peace and War: A Theory of International Relations*, trans. R. Howard and A. Baker Fox, Garden City, NY: Doubleday.

Asiegbu, Johnson U. J. (1969) *Slavery and the Politics of Liberation, 1787–1861: A study of liberated African emigration and British anti-slavery policy*, London: Longman.

— (1984): *Nigeria and Its British Invaders*, New York: Nok Publishers International.

Atlantic Charter, The (1941) www.archives.gov/education/lessons/fdr-churchill/images/atlantic-charter.gif, accessed 13 January 2011.

Barrientos, A. and J. De Jong (2006) 'Reducing child poverty with cash transfers: a sure thing?', *Development Policy Review*, XXIV(5): 537–52.

Bartkus, V. O. (1999) *The Dynamic of Secession*, Cambridge: Cambridge University Press.

Bassett, T. J. (2010) 'Slim pickings: Fairtrade Cotton in West Africa', *Geoforum*, XLI(1): 44–55.

Bates, R. H. (1981) *Markets and States in Tropical Africa: The political basis of agricultural policies*, Berkeley: University of California Press.

Bauer, G. and S. D. Taylor (2005) *Politics in Southern Africa: State and Society in Transition*, Boulder, CO: Lynne Rienner.

Bay, E. and N. Hafkin (eds) (1976) *Women in Africa: Studies in Social and Economic Change*, Stanford, CA: Stanford University Press.

Beckmann, N. and J. Bujra (2010) 'The politics of the queue: PLHA politicisation and AIDS activism in Tanzania', *Development and Change*, XLI(6): 1041–64.

Berber, I. and E. F. White (1999) *Women in sub-Saharan African: Restoring Women to History*, Bloomington and Indianapolis: Indiana University Press.

Bernal, M. (1991) *Black Athena: The Afroasiatic Roots of Classical Civilization*, Chapel Hill, NC: Rutgers University Press.

Blackie, M. (2006) 'Are fertilizer subsidies necessary?', in T. Woods and L. Daniel (eds), *Achieving Food Security: What next for sub-Saharan Africa?*, Brighton: Institute for Development Studies.

Blundo, G. and J.-P. Olivier de Sardan (eds) (2006) *Everyday Corruption and the State: Citizen and public officials in Africa*, London: Zed Books.

Boesten, J. (2009) 'Transactable sex and unsafe practices: gender and sex when living with HIV/AIDS', in J. Boesten and N. Poku (eds), *Gender and HIV/AIDS: Critical perspectives from the Developing World*, Aldershot: Ashgate.

Boesten, J., A. Mdee and F. Cleaver (2011) 'Service delivery on the cheap? Community-based workers in Development Interventions', *Development in Practice* (forthcoming).

Borras, S. and J. Franco (2010) 'From threat to opportunity? Problems with the idea of a "code of conduct" for land grabbing', *Yale Human Rights and Development*, XIII: 507–23.

Boserup, E. (1970) *Women's Role in Economic Development*, New York: Allen and Unwin.

Bowers, J. K. and P. Cheshire (1983) *Agriculture, the Countryside and Land Use: An economic critique*, London: Methuen.

Broekhuis, A. and H. Huisman (2001) 'Resettlement revisited: land reform results in resource-poor regions in Zimbabwe', *Geoforum*, XXXII: 285–98.

Bryceson, D. (1995) 'Wishful thinking: theory and practice of Western donor efforts to raise women's status in rural Africa', in D. Bryceson (ed.), *Cross-Cultural Perspectives on Women*, vol. XVI: *Women Wielding the Hoe: Lessons from rural Africa for feminist theory and development practice*, Oxford: Berg.

— (2000) *Rural Africa at the Cross-roads: Livelihoods, practices and policies*, Natural Resource Perspectives no. 52, London: Overseas Development Institute.

— (2004) 'Agrarian vista or vortex: African rural livelihood policies', *Review of African Political Economy*, XXXI(102): 617–29.

Bujra, J. (2003) 'Targeting men for a change: AIDS discourse and activism in Africa', in F. Cleaver (ed.), *Masculinities Matter: Men, Gender and Development*, London: Zed Books.

Busia, K. A. (1967) *Africa in Search of Democracy*, London: Routledge and Kegan Paul.

Buvé, A., K. Bishikwabo-Nzarhaza and G. Mutangadura (2002) 'The spread and effect of HIV-1 infection in sub-Saharan Africa', *The Lancet*, CCCLIX(9322): 2011–17.

Buvinic, M. (1986) 'Projects for women in the Third World: explaining their misbehaviour', *World Development*, XIV(5): 653–64.

Buvinic, M., L. A. Margaret and M. William (1978) *Women and Poverty in the Third World*, Baltimore, MD: Johns Hopkins University Press.

Caldwell, J., P. Caldwell and P. Quiggin (1989) 'The social context of AIDS in sub-Saharan Africa', *Population and Development Review*, XV(2): 185–234.

Carr, E. (2008) 'Men's crops and women's crops: the importance of gender in the understanding of agricultural and development outcomes in Ghana's Central Region', *World Development*, XXXVI(5): 900–915.

Chabal, P. (2009) *Africa: The Politics*

of *Suffering and Smiling*, London: Zed Books.

Chant, S. (2007) *Gender, Generation and Poverty. Exploring the 'Feminisation of Poverty' in Africa, Asia and Latin America*, Cheltenham: Edward Elgar.

Chinsinga, B. (2005) 'The clash of voices: community-based targeting of safety-net interventions in Malawi', *Social Policy and Administration*, XXXIX(3): 284–301.

— (2008) *The Malawi Agricultural Subsidy Programme: Politics and pragmatism*, Future Agricultures Briefing, February.

Chirimuuta, R. and R. (1989) *AIDS, Africa and Racism*, London: Free Association Books.

Clapham, C. (1990) *Transformation and Continuity in Revolutionary Ethiopia*, 2nd edn, Cambridge: Cambridge University Press.

Clausewitz, C. V. (1942) *The Principles of War*, trans. and ed. Hans W. Gatzke, Military Service Publishing Company.

Clay, E. (2006) 'Is food aid effective?', in T. Woods and L. Daniel (eds), *Achieving Food Security: What next for sub-Saharan Africa?*, Brighton: Institute for Development Studies, April.

Cleaver, F. (ed.) (2003) *Masculinities Matter! Men, Gender and Development*, London: Zed Books.

— (2005) 'The inequality of social capital and the reproduction of chronic poverty', *World Development*, XXXIII(6): 893–906.

Cleaver, F. and A. Toner (2006) 'The evolution of community water governance in Uchira, Tanzania: the implications for equality of access, sustainability and effectiveness', *Natural Resources Forum*, XXX(3): 207–18.

Coles, A. and T. Wallace (eds) (2005) *Gender, Water and Development*, Oxford: Berg.

Collier, P. (1999) 'On the economic consequences of civil war', *Oxford Economic Papers*, LI(1): 168–83.

Collier, P. and J.-W. Gunning (1999) *The IMF's Role in Structural Adjustment*, Oxford: Centre for Study of African Economies.

Collier, P., G. Conway and T. Venables (2008) 'Climate change and Africa', *Oxford Review of Economic Policy*, XXIV(2): 337–53.

Collier, P., A. Hoeffler and C. Pattillo (2004) 'Africa's exodus: capital flight and the brain drain as portfolio decisions', *Journal of African Economies*, Supplement 2, XIII(0): 15–54.

Commission on HIV/AIDS and Governance in Africa (2004) *Speech by H. E. Girma W/Giorgis, President of the Federal Democratic Republic of Ethiopia*, Addis Ababa, 14 October, www.uneca.org/chga/speech_girma.htm, accessed 13 January 2011.

Comprehensive Africa Agriculture Development Programme (2010) www.nepad-caadp.net, accessed 13 January 2011.

Conference at Berlin (1884) *General Act of the Conference at Berlin*, www.thelatinlibrary.com/imperialism/readings/berlinconference.html, accessed 13 January 2011.

Conning, J. and M. Kevane (2002) 'Community-based targeting mechanisms for social safety nets: a critical review', *World Development*, XXX(3): 375–94.

Coovadia, H., R. Jewkes, P. Barron, D. Sanders and D. McIntyre (2009) 'Health in South Africa: the health and health system of South Africa: historical roots of current public health challenges', *The Lancet*, CCCLXXIV(9692): 817–34.

Cornwall, A. (2003) 'Whose voices? Whose choices? Reflections on gender and participatory development', *World Development*, XXXI(8): 1325–42.

Cornwall, A. and S. White (2000) 'Introduction: men, masculinities and development: politics, policies and practice', *IDS Bulletin*, XXXI(2): 1–6.

Cotula, L., S. Vermeulen, R. Leonard and J. Keeley (2009) *Land Grab or Development Opportunity? Agricultural investment and international land deals in Africa*, London and Rome: International Institute for Environment and Development/Food and Agriculture Organization/International Fund for Agricultural Development.

Cousins, B. and I. Scoones (2009). 'Contested paradigms of "viability" in redistributive land reform: perspectives from southern Africa', Working paper for Livelihoods after Land Reform Project, Brighton: Institute of Development Studies.

Crush, J. and B. Frayne (2010) *Surviving on the Move: Migration, poverty and development in Southern Africa*, Cape Town: Idasa Publishing.

Dauber, R. and M. Cain (eds) (1981) *Women and Technological Change in Developing Countries*, Boulder, CO: Westview Press.

Davidson, B. (1964) *Which Way Africa: The Search for a New Society*, London: Penguin.

— (1978) *Africa in Modern History: The Search for a New Society*, London: Penguin.

Debt Crisis Network Staff (1985) *From Debt to Development: Alternatives to the International Debt Crisis*, Washington, DC: Institute for Policy Studies.

Delius, P. and L. Walker (2002) 'AIDS in context', *African Studies*, LXI(1): 5–13.

Denov, M. (2006) 'Wartime sexual violence: assessing a human security response to war-affected girls in Sierra Leone', *Security Dialogue*, XXXVII: 319–42.

Denton, F. (2002) 'Climate change vulnerability, impacts, and adaptation: why does gender matter?', *Gender and Development*, X(2): 10–20.

Department for International Development (DfID) (2004) *Agriculture, Growth and Poverty Reduction*, London: Department for International Development.

Development Alternatives with Women for a New Era (DAWN) (1985) *Development, Crisis, and Alternative Visions*, Oslo: Media-Redaksjonen.

Devereux, S., B. Vaitla and S. H. Swan (2008) *Seasons of Hunger: Fighting cycles of quiet starvation among the World's rural poor*, Chippenham and Eastbourne: Pluto Press.

Dolan, C. (2003) 'Collapsing masculinities and weak states: a case study of northern Uganda', in F. Cleaver (ed.), *Masculinities Matter! Men, Gender and Development*, London: Zed Books.

Dorward, A., P. Hazell and C. Poulton (2008) *Rethinking Agricultural Input Subsidies in Poor Rural Economies*, Future Agricultures Briefing, Brighton: Future Agricultures Consortium, February.

Doss, C. (2001) 'Designing agricultural technology for African women farmers: lessons from 25 years of experience', *World Development*, XXIX(12): 2075–92.

Du Bois, W. E. B. (1964) *Black Reconstruction in America*, New York: Meridian Books.

Easterly, W. (2009) 'How the Millennium Development Goals are unfair to Africa', *World Development*, XXXVII(1): 26–35.

Ellis, A. (2007) *Gender and Economic Growth in Kenya. Unleashing the Power of Women*, Washington, DC: World Bank.

Ellis, F. (2000) *Rural Livelihoods and Diversity in Developing Countries*, Oxford: Oxford University Press.

Elson, D. (ed.) (1991) *The Male Bias in the Development Process*, Manchester: Manchester University Press.

Epstein, H. (2005) 'God and the fight against AIDS', *New York Review of Books*, LII(7): 47–51.

— (2007) *The Invisible Cure: Africa, the West, and the fight against AIDS*, New York: Farrar, Straus & Giroux.

Eze, E. C. (1997) *Postcolonial African Philosophy: A critical reader*, Cambridge: Blackwell.

Famine Early Warning Systems Network (FEWS NET) (2009) *Southern Africa Food Security Update*, December 2008/January 2009, www.fews.net/docs/Publications/south_2009_01.pdf, accessed 13 January 2011.

Fanon, F. (1961) *The Wretched of the Earth*, Paris: Maspero.

Fieldhouse, D. K. (1986) *Black Africa 1945–1980: Economic Decolonisation and Arrested Development*, London: Unwin Hyman.

Food and Agriculture Organization of the United Nations (FAO) (2008) *Linking Social Protection and Support to Small Farmer Development*, Rome: FAO.

— (2009) *The State of Food Insecurity in the World: Economic crises –* impacts and lessons learned, Rome: FAO.

Fosu, A. K. (1991) 'Capital instability and economic growth in sub-Saharan Africa', *Journal of Development Studies*, XXVIII(1): 74–85.

Fosu, A. K. and P. Collier (eds) (2005) *Post-Conflict Economies in Africa*, New York: Palgrave Macmillan.

Future Agricultures (2008) *The Malawi Agricultural Subsidy Programme: Politics and pragmatism*, Future Agricultures Briefing, Policy Brief 022, Brighton: Future Agricultures Consortium, February.

Gates Foundation (2009) *Agricultural Development: Strategy Overview*, Seattle, WA: Bill and Melinda Gates Foundation.

Gehab, K., S. Kalloch, M. Medard, A.-T. Nyapendi, C. Lywenya and M. Kyangwa (2008) 'Nile perch and the hungry of Lake Victoria: gender, status and food in an East African fishery', *Food Policy*, XXXIII(1): 85–98.

Geisler, G. (2000) '"Parliament is another terrain of struggle": women, men and politics in South Africa', *Journal of Modern African Studies*, XXXVIII(4): 605–30.

Gizelis, T. (2009) 'Gender and United Nations peacebuilding', *Journal of Peace Research*, XLI(4): 505–23.

Glennie, J. (2008) *The Trouble with Aid: Why Less Could Mean More for Africa*, London: Zed Books.

Glynn, J. R., M. Caraël, B. Auvert, M. Kahindo, J. Chege, R. Musonda, F. Kaona and A. Buvé (2001) 'Why do young women have a much higher prevalence of HIV than young men? A study in Kisumu, Kenya and Ndola, Zambia', *AIDS*, XV(4): 51–60.

Goetz, A. M. (1991) 'Feminism and the claim to know: contradictions in feminist approaches to women in development', in R. Grant and K. Newland (eds), *Gender and International Relations*, Bloomington: Indiana University Press.

Gosling, L. and D. Cohen (2007) *Advocacy Matters: Helping Children to Change Their World*, London: International Save the Children Alliance.

Gowing, J. W. and M. Palmer (2008) 'Sustainable agricultural development in sub-Saharan Africa: the case for a paradigm shift in land husbandry', *Soil Use and Management*, XXIV: 92–9.

Gray, R., N. Kiwanuka, T. C. Quinn, N. K. Sewankambo, D. Serwadda, F. W. Mangen, T. Lutalo, F. Nalugoda, R. Kelly, M. Meehan, M. Z. Chen, C. Li and M. J. Wawer (2000) 'Male circumcision and HIV acquisition and transmission: cohort studies in Rakai, Uganda', *AIDS*, XIV(15): 2371–81.

Green, D. (2008) *From Poverty to Power: How active citizens and effective states can change the world*, Oxford: Oxfam.

Green, E. (1994) *AIDS and STDs in Africa*, Boulder, CO: Westview Press.

Gregson, S., C. A. Nyamukapa, G. P. Garnett, P. R. Mason, T. Zhuwau, M. Caraël, S. K. Chandiwana and R. M. Anderson (2002) 'Sexual mixing patterns and sex-differentials in teenage exposure to HIV infection in rural Zimbabwe', *The Lancet*, CCCLIX(9321): 1896–1903.

Griffiths, P. (2003) *The Economist's Tale*, London: Zed Books.

Gubhaju, B. and G. F. De Jong (2009) 'Individual versus household migration decisions rules: gender and marital status differences in intentions to migrate in South Africa', *International Migration*, XLVII(1): 31–60.

Hailey, Lord (1961) *An African Survey – a Study of Problems Arising in Africa South of the Sahara*, Oxford: Oxford University Press.

Hampel-Milagrosa, A. and J. Frickenstein (2008) 'Taking the women's perspective: gender risks of regulatory reforms in sub-Saharan Africa', *Enterprise Development and Microfinance*, XIX(3): 1755–78.

Harries, A., R. Zachariah, K. Tayler-Smith, E. Schouten, F. Chimbwandira, W. Van Damme and M. El-Sadr (2010) 'Keeping health facilities safe: one way of strengthening the interaction between disease-specific programmes and health systems', *Tropical Medicine and International Health*, XV(12): 1407–12.

Harrigan, J. (2003) 'U-turns and full circles: two decades of agricultural reform in Malawi 1981–2000', *World Development*, XXXI(5): 847–63.

Hazell, P., C. Poulton, S. Wiggins and A. Dorward (2007) 'The future of small farms for poverty reduction and growth', 2020 Discussion Papers, Washington, DC: International Food Policy Research Institute.

Hegel, G. W. F. (1956) *The Philosophy of History*, Mineola, NY: Dover Publications.

Herbst, J. (2000) *States and Power in Africa: Comparative lessons in authority and control*, Princeton, NJ: Princeton University Press.

Hickey, S. and G. Mohan (eds) (2004) *Participation: From Tyranny to Transformation*, London: Zed Books.

Hine, R., J. Pretty and S. Twarog (2008) *Organic Agriculture and Food Security in Africa*, New York and Geneva: United Nations

Conference on Trade and Development/United Nations Environment Programme.

Hobbes, T. (1968) *Leviathan*, ed. C. B. Macpherson, Harmondsworth: Penguin.

Holt-Giménez, E. and R. Patel (2009) *Food Rebellions: Crisis and the hunger for justice*, Oxford: Pambazuka Press.

Human Sciences Research Council (2008) *South African National HIV Prevalence, Incidence, Behaviour and Communication Survey: A turning tide among teenagers?*, Cape Town: HRSC Press.

Ijeoma, A. N. and U. Nkiru (2008) 'Legislating gender, (re)producing rights: an analysis of African case law', *Journal of Social Welfare and Family Law*, XXX(2): 117–26.

Integrated Regional Information Networks (IRIN) (2008) *Malawi: Subsidising agriculture is not enough*, Johannesburg, 5 February, www.irinnews.org/Report. aspx?ReportId=76591, accessed 13 January 2011.

— (2009) *Africa: Agriculture an underestimated 'safety net'*, Johannesburg, 9 June, irinnews. org/Report.aspx?ReportId=84777, accessed 13 January 2011.

International Food Policy Research Institute (IFPRI) (2009) *2009 Global Hunger Index: The Challenge of Hunger: Focus on Financial Crisis and Gender Inequality*, Washington, DC: International Food Policy Research Institute.

International Monetary Fund (IMF) (1998) *Annual Report 1998*, Washington, DC: International Monetary Fund.

International Organization for Migration (IOM) (2003) *Mobile Populations and HIV/AIDS in the Southern Africa Region: Recommendations for action*, Pretoria: International Organization for Migration.

Irz, X., L. Lin, C. Thirtle and S. Wiggins (2001) 'Agricultural productivity growth and poverty alleviation', *Development Policy Review*, XIX(4): 449–66.

Izumi, K. (1999) 'Liberalisation, gender, and the land question in sub-Saharan Africa', *Gender and Development*, VII(3): 9–18.

Jacobson, R. (2006) 'Mozambique and the construction of gendered agency in war', *Women's Studies International Forum*, XXVI(5): 499–509.

Jazairy, I., M. Alamgir and T. Panuccio (1992) *The State of World Rural Poverty: An enquiry into its causes and consequences*, London: Intermediate Technology Publications for IFAD.

Jewkes, R., C. Vundule and F. E. A. Maforah (2001) 'Relationship dynamics and teenage pregnancy in South Africa', *Social Science and Medicine*, LII(5): 733–44.

Johnson-Sirleaf, E. (2009) *This Child Will Be Great: Memoir of a Remarkable Life by Africa's First Woman President*, New York: HarperCollins.

Kabeer, N. (2005) 'Gender equality and women's empowerment: a critical analysis of the Third Millennium Development Goal', *Gender and Development*, XIII(1): 13–24.

Kalichman, S. (2009) *Denying AIDS: Conspiracy Theories, Pseudoscience, and Human Tragedy*, New York: Copernicus Books.

Kamali, A., M. Quigley, J. Nakiyingi, J. Kinsman, J. Kengeya-Kayondo, R. Gopal, A. Ojwiya, P. Hughes,

L. M. Carpenter and J. Whitworth (2003) 'Syndromic management of sexually-transmitted infections and behaviour change interventions on transmission of HIV-1 in rural Uganda: a community randomised trial', *The Lancet*, CCCLXI(9358): 645–52.

Kark, S. L. (1949) 'The social pathology of syphilis in Africans', *South African Medical Journal*, XXIII: 77–84, reprinted in *International Journal of Epidemiology* (2003), XXXII(2): 181–6.

Kayizzi-Mugerwa, S. (ed.) (2003) *Reforming Africa's Institutions: Ownership, Incentives, and Capabilities*, Tokyo: United Nations University Press.

Keen, D. (2005) *Conflict and Collusion in Sierra Leone*, Basingstoke: Palgrave.

Keller, B. and B. C. Mbwewe (1991) 'Policy planning for the empowerment of Zambia's women farmers', *Canadian Journal of Development Studies*, XII(1): 75–88.

King, C. (2008) 'Community resilience and contemporary agri-ecological systems: reconnecting people and food, and people with people', *Systems Research and Behavioural Science*, XXV: 111–24.

Kinsey, B. (2004) 'Zimbabwe's Land Reform Program: underinvestment in post-conflict transformation', *World Development*, XXXII(10): 1669–96.

Langyintuo, A. S. (2005) *Maize Production Systems in Malawi: Setting indicators for impact assessment and targeting*, Harare: International Maize and Wheat Improvement Centre (CIMMYT).

Leavy, J. and H. White (2006) 'Maize production in Zambia', in T. Woods and L. Daniel (eds), *Achieving Food Security: What next for sub-Saharan Africa?*, Brighton: Institute for Development Studies, April.

Legum, C. (1961) *Congo Disaster*, London: Penguin.

Lingard, J. (2002) *Agricultural Subsidies and Environmental Change*, Newcastle upon Tyne: John Wiley and Sons.

Lloyd, C. and P. Hewett (2009) 'Educational inequalities in the midst of persistent poverty: diversity across Africa in educational outcomes', *Journal of International Development*, XXI(8): 1137–51.

Lurie, M. N., B. G. Williams, K. Zuma, D. Mkaya-Mwamburi, G. P. Garnett, M. D. Sweat, J. Gittelsohn and S. S. Karim (2003) 'Who infects whom? HIV-1 concordance and discordance among migrant and non-migrant couples in South Africa', *AIDS*, XVII(15): 2245–52.

Maene, L. M. (2000) *Agricultural Subsidies in Developed Countries – an Overview*, Seminar presentation, New Delhi, 11–13 December, Paris: International Fertilizer Industry Association, www.fertilizer.org/ifa/Home-Page/LIBRARY/Publication-database.html/Agricultural-Subsidies-in-Developed-Countries-An-Overview.html, accessed 13 January 2011.

Maizels, M. (1994) *Commodity Markets Trends and Instability: Policy options for developing countries*, Geneva: United Nations Conference on Trade and Development.

Malawi Vulnerability Assessment Committee (MVAC) (2005) *Malawi Vulnerability Assessment Committee Report*, ochaonline.un.org/rosa/FoodSecurity/tabid/5034/language/en-US/Default.aspx, accessed 13 January 2011.

Mamdani, M. (1996) *Citizen and*

Subject: Contemporary Africa and the Legacy of Late Colonialism, Kampala: Fountain Publishers.

Marchand, M. H. and J. L. Parpart (eds) (1995) *Feminism, Postmodernism and Development*, New York: Routledge.

Martin-Prével, Y., F. Delpeuch, P. Traissac, J. P. Massamba, G. Adoua-Oyila, K. Coudert and S. Trèche (2000) 'Deterioration in the nutritional status of young children and their mothers in Brazzaville, Congo, following the 1994 devaluation of the CFA franc', *World Health Bulletin*, LXXVIII(1): 108–18.

Masina, L. (2007) 'Malawi: Malawi donates surplus food', *African Business*, 336: 68–70.

Matume, G. (2004) 'Women break into African politics: quota systems allow more women to gain elected office', *Africa Recovery*, XVIII(1), April.

Mayrand, K., S. Dionne, M. Paquin and I. Pageot-LeBel (2003) 'The economic and environmental impacts of agricultural subsidies: an assessment of the 2002 US Farm Bill & Doha Round', Draft paper, Unisfera International Centre, Montreal, www.cec.org/files/PDF/ECONOMY/Eco-Envi-Impacts-Agric-Subsidies_en.pdf, accessed 13 January 2011.

McGowan, P. J. (2003) 'African military coups d'état, 1956–2001: frequency, trends and distribution', *Journal of Modern African Studies*, XXIV(3): 539–46.

Meinzen-Dick, R., M. Adato, L. Haddad and P. Hazell (2004) *Science and Poverty: An Interdisciplinary Assessment of the Impact of Agricultural Research*, Food Policy Report no. 16, Washington, DC:

International Food Policy Research Institute (IFPRI).

Mercer, C. (2002) 'The discourse of Maendeleo and the politics of women's participation on Mount Kilimanjaro', *Development and Change*, XXXIII(1): 101–28.

Midwinter, E. (2006) 'Salisbury', *British Prime Ministers of the 20th Century*, London: Haus Publishers.

Minujin, A. and E. Delamonica (2003) 'Mind the gap! Widening child mortality disparities', *Journal of Human Development*, IV(3): 396–418.

Mkandawire, R. and K. Albright (2006) 'Editorial', in T. Woods and L. Daniel (eds), *Achieving Food Security: What next for sub-Saharan Africa?*, Brighton: Institute for Development Studies, April.

Mkandawire, T. and C. Soludo (1999) *Our Continent, Our Future: African Perspectives on Structural Adjustment*, Trenton, NJ: Africa World Press.

Mkwambisi, D. D. (2009) 'Urban agriculture and food security in Lilongwe and Blantyre, Malawi', in M. Redwood (ed.), *Agriculture in Urban Planning: Generating livelihoods and food security*, London: Earthscan and the International Development Research Centre (IDRC).

Momsen, J. (2001) 'Backlash: or how to snatch failure from the jaws of success in gender and development progress', *Progress in Development*, I(1): 253–60.

Morna, C. (2007) 'Making every voice count: a southern Africa case study', *Gender and Development*, XV(3): 369–85.

Mosse, D. (2001) 'People's knowledge, participation and patronage: operations and representations in rural development', in B. Cooke and U. Kothari, *Participation: The New Tyranny?*, London: Zed Books.

Moyo, D. (2009) *Dead Aid: Why Aid Is Not Working and How There Is a Better Way for Africa*, New York: Farrar, Straus & Giroux.

Muhumuza, F. (2002) 'A livelihoods-grounded audit of the Plan for the Modernisation of Agriculture (PMA) in Uganda', Working Paper no. 14, Goodbye to Projects, Bradford Centre for International Development, Bradford.

Murphy, C. (1999) *Cultivating Havana: Urban agriculture and food security in the years of crisis*, Oakland, CA: Institute for Food and Development Policy.

Mwangwela, A. M. (2001) 'The role of Bunda College of Agriculture in the post harvest sector in Malawi', Paper presented at the FAO-GFAR Global Initiative for Postharvest Technology meeting, 17–19 September, Entebbe.

Nagayets, O. (2005) *Small Farms: Current status and key trends*, Information brief prepared for the Future of Small Farms Research Workshop, Wye College, 26–29 June.

Newitt, M. (1981) *Portugal in Africa: The Last 100 Years*, Harlow: Longman.

Nkrumah, K. (1957) *Towards Colonial Freedom: Africa in the Struggle against World Imperialism*, London: PANAF Books.

Nnaemeka, O. and J. Ezeilo (eds) (2005) *Engendering Human Rights: Cultural and Socio-economic Realities in Africa*, Basingstoke: Palgrave Macmillan.

Nyerere, J. (1968) *Ujamaa: Essays on Socialism*, Oxford: Oxford University Press.

— (1984) 3rd World Conference on Women: African Preparatory Conference.

Nzenza-Shand, S. (2005) 'Take me back to the village: African women and the dynamics of health and human rights in Tanzania and Zimbabwe', in O. Nnaemeka and J. Ezeilo (eds), *Engendering Human Rights: Cultural and Socio-economic Realities in Africa*, Basingstoke: Palgrave Macmillan.

Obbo, C. (2003) 'Cultural and religious sensibilities and behavioural change', UNAIDS project paper for AIDS in Africa Scenarios, Joint United Nations Programme on HIV/AIDS (UNAIDS), Geneva.

Odame, H. H. (2002) 'Men in women's groups', in F. Cleaver (ed.), *Masculinity Matters: Men and Development*, London: Zed Books.

Orock, R. T. E. (2007) 'Gender equality: whose agenda? Observations from Cameroon', *Development in Practice*, XVII(1): 93–7.

Owen, R. and B. Sutcliffe (eds) (1972) *Studies in the Theory of Imperialism*, London.

Peters, P. (2009) 'Challenges in land tenure and land reform in Africa: anthropological contributions', *World Development*, XXXVII(8): 1317–25.

Peters, P. E. (2006) 'Rural income and poverty in a time of radical change in Malawi', *Journal of Development Studies*, XLII(2): 322–45.

Pisani E. (2003) 'The epidemiology of HIV at the start of the 21st century: reviewing the evidence', Working paper, United Nations Children's Fund (UNICEF), New York, September.

— (2008) *The Wisdom of Whores: Bureaucrats, Brothels and the*

Business of AIDS, London: Granta Books.

Place, F. (2009) 'Land tenure and agricultural productivity in Africa: a comparative analysis of the economic literature and recent policy reforms', *World Development*, XXXVII(8): 1326–36.

Platteau, J.-P. (2004) 'Monitoring elite capture in community-driven development', *Development and Change*, 35(2): 223–46.

Platteau, J.-P. and F. Gaspart (2003) 'The risk of resource misappropriation in community-driven development', *World Development*, XXXI(10): 1687–703.

Poku, N. K. (2006) *AIDS in Africa: How the poor are dying*, Cambridge: Polity Press.

— (2013) *Africa and HIV/AIDS: Impact, Resilience and Change*, Cambridge: Cambridge University Press (forthcoming).

Poku, N. and A. Mdee (2010) Interview with General Olusegun Obasanjo, 17 December 2010, London (unpublished).

Poku, N. K. and J. Whitman (2011) 'The Millennium Development Goals and development after 2015', *Third World Quarterly*, XI (forthcoming).

Poku, N. K., A. Whiteside and B. Sandkjaer (eds) (2007) *AIDS and Governance*, Aldershot: Ashgate.

Ponte, S. (1999) 'Trading images: discourse and statistical evidence on agricultural adjustment in Tanzania (1986–95)', in P. G. Forster and S. Maghimbi (eds), *Agrarian Economy, State and Society in Contemporary Tanzania*, Aldershot: Ashgate.

Post, K. (1964) *The New States of West Africa*, Harlow: Penguin.

Pretty, J. N., J. Morison and E. Hine (2003) 'Reducing food poverty by increasing agricultural sustainability in developing countries', *Agriculture, Ecosystems and Environment*, XCV(1): 217–34.

Rajan, R. (2010) *Fault Lines: How Hidden Fractures Still Threaten the World Economy*, London: Princeton University Press.

Ranger, T. (1996) 'Colonial and post-colonial identities', in R. Werbner and T. Ranger (eds), *Postcolonial Identities in Africa*, London: Zed Books.

Rao, J. (2009) 'Challenges facing world agriculture: a political economy perspective', *Development and Change*, XL(6): 1279–92.

Rathgeber, E. M. (1995) 'Gender and development in action', in M. H. Marchand and J. L. Parpart (eds), *Feminism, Postmodernism and Development*, New York: Routledge.

Ravillion, M. (2009) 'Are there lessons for Africa from China's success against poverty?', *World Development*, XXXVI(2): 303–13.

Razavi, S. (2007) 'Liberalisation and the debates on women's access to land', *Third World Quarterly*, XXVIII(8): 1479–500.

Resilience Alliance (n.d.) *Key Concepts: Resilience* (web page), www.resalliance.org/index.php/resilience, accessed 13 January 2011.

Rice, X. (2010) 'Ethiopia – country of the silver sickle – offers land dirt cheap to farming giants', *Guardian*, 15 January, www.guardian.co.uk/world/2010/jan/15/ethiopia-sells-land-farming-giants, accessed 13 January 2011.

Riley, S. P. and T. W. Parfitt (1994) 'Economic adjustment and democratization in Africa', in J. Walton and D. Seddon, *Free*

Markets and Food Riots: The Politics of Global Adjustment, Oxford: Blackwell.

Rockström, J. (2003) 'Resilience building and water demand management for drought mitigation', *Physics and Chemistry of the Earth*, XXVIII: 869–77.

Rogers, B. (1981) *The Domestication of Women: Discrimination in Developing Societies*, Oxford: Routledge.

Rosset, P. and M. Bourque (2005) 'Lessons of Cuban resistance', in J. N. Pretty (ed.), *The Earthscan Reader on Sustainable Development*, London: Earthscan.

Rothchild, D. and O. Victor (eds) (1983) *State vs Ethnic Claims: African Policy Dilemmas*, Boulder, CO: Westview Press.

Royal Agricultural Society of England (RASE) (2000) *Routes to Rural Poverty: Farmland management strategies for the UK*, Warwickshire: Communications Department, Royal Agricultural Society of England.

Rugimbana, R. and A. Spring (2009) 'Marketing micro-finance to women: integrating global with local', *International Journal of Nonprofit and Voluntary Sector Marketing*, XIV(2): 149–54.

Rushton, J. P. and A. F. Bogaert (1989) 'Population differences in susceptibility to AIDS: an evolutionary analysis', *Social Science and Medicine*, XXVIII(12): 1211–20.

Sachs, J. (2005) *The End of Poverty*, London: Penguin.

Said, E. (1979) *Orientalism*, London: Vintage.

Sanchez, P. A., A.-M. N. Izac, R. J. Buresh, K. D. Shepherd, M. Soule, C. A. Palm, P. L. Woomer and C. G. Nderitu (1997) 'Soil fertility replenishment in Africa as an investment in natural resource management', in R. J. Buresh and P. A. Sanchez (eds), *Recapitalization of Soil Nutrient Capital in Sub-Saharan Africa*, Madison, WI: ASSA/CSSA/SSSA.

Sartre, J. P. (1979) *Black Orpheus*, Paris: Gallimard.

Scoones, I. (2009) 'Livelihoods perspectives and rural development', *Journal of Peasant Studies*, XXXVI(1): 171–96.

Scott, J. (1999) *Seeing Like a State: How Certain Schemes to Improve the Human Condition Have Failed*, London: Yale University Press.

Senghor, L. (1950) *Nationhood and the African Road to Socialism*, Paris: Presence Africaine.

Smith, G. D. (2009) 'East Africa: extended families with many rights', *Entrepreneurship Theory and Practice*, XXXIII: 1239–44.

Smith, R. M. (2002) 'Modern citizenship', in E. F. Isin and B. S. Turner (eds), *Handbook of Citizenship Studies*, London: Sage.

Sokile, C. S., J. J. Kashaigili and R. M. J. Kadigi (2003) 'Towards an integrated water resource management in Tanzania: the role of an appropriate institutional framework in Rufiji Basin', *Physics and Chemistry of the Earth*, 28(20–27): 1015–23.

Staatz, J. and N. Dembélé (2007) 'Agriculture for development in sub-Saharan Africa', Background paper for the *World Development Report 2008*, Washington, DC: World Bank.

Stamp, P. (1989) *Technology, Gender, and Power in Africa*, Technical Study 63E, Ottawa: International Development Research Centre.

Stanford University (2009) 'Massive imbalances found in global fertilizer use, resulting in malnourishment in some areas and serious pollution problems in others', Reprinted in *Science Daily*, 8 July, www.sciencedaily.com / releases/2009/06/090618144000.htm, accessed 13 January 2011.

Staudt, K. (1985) *Women, Foreign Assistance and Advocacy Administration*, New York: Praeger.

Stedman, S. J. (ed.) (1993) *Botswana: The political economy of democratic development*, Boulder, CO: Lynne Rienner.

Stephenson, J. M. and F. M. Cowan (2003) 'Evaluating interventions for HIV prevention in Africa', *The Lancet*, CCCLXI: 633–4.

Stewart, F. (1995) *Adjustment and Poverty: Options and Choices*, London: Routledge.

Stoneburner, R. L. and D. Low-Beer (2004) 'Population-level HIV declines and behavioral risk avoidance in Uganda', *Science*, CCCIV: 714–18.

Streefland, P. (2001) 'Public doubts about vaccination safety and resistance against vaccination', *Health Policy*, LV(3): 159–72.

Tamale, S. (2000) '"Point of order, Mr Speaker": African women claiming their space in parliament', *Gender and Development*, VIII(3): 8–15.

Tinker, I. (1990) 'The making of a field: advocates, practitioners and scholars', in I. Tinker (ed.), *Persistent Inequalities: Women and World Development*, Oxford: Oxford University Press.

Toner, A. (2008) 'Who shapes development? An ethnography of participation in collective village life in Uchira, Tanzania', Unpublished PhD thesis, University of Bradford.

Toulmin, C. (2009) *Climate Change in Africa*, London: Zed Books.

Toulmin, C. and J. Quan (2000) *Evolving Land Rights, Policy and Tenure in Africa*, London: Department for International Development (DfID)/ International Institute for Environment and Development (IIED)/ Natural Resources Institute (NRI).

Townsend, R. F. (1999) *Agricultural Incentives in sub-Saharan Africa: Policy challenges*, Washington, DC: World Bank.

Udahemuka, S. (2009) '"End of poverty"? An exploration of the Millennium Villages project in sub-Saharan Africa', Unpublished PhD Thesis, University of Bradford.

Ugandan AIDS Commission (2000) *HIV/AIDS in Uganda: A summary of impact, prevalence and national strategies*, Kampala: Ugandan AIDS Commission.

UK Food Group (2008) *More Aid for African Agriculture: Policy implications for small-scale farmers*, Report, London: UK Food Group.

UNCTAD (United Nations Conference on Trade and Development) (2006) *The Least Developed Countries 2006 Report*, Geneva: United Nations Commission on Trade and Development.

— (2010) *World Investment Report*, New York: United Nations Press.

United Nations (UN) (1996) *The United Nations and the Advancement of Women, 1945–1996*, New York: United Nations.

— (2001) *World Economic and Social Survey 2000*, New York: Department of Economic and Social Affairs, United Nations.

— (2008) *Millennium Development Goals Report*, New York: United Nations.

— (2009) *World Survey on the Role of Women in Development*, New York: United Nations.

— (2010) *The Millennium Development Goals Report*, New York:
United Nations.

United Nations Children's Fund
(UNICEF) (1987) *Adjustment with
a Human Face*, 2 vols, Oxford:
Oxford University Press.

United Nations Development
Programme (UNDP) (2007) *Human
Development Report 2007/2008:
Fighting climate change: human
solidarity in a divided world*,
Basingstoke: Palgrave Macmillan.

— (2009) *Overcoming Barriers:
Human Mobility and Development*,
Human Development Report
2009, New York: United Nations
Development Programme.

— (2010) *African Development Report
2010*, New York: United Nations
Development Programme.

United Nations Secretary-General's
Task Force on Women, Girls and
HIV/AIDS in Southern Africa
(2004) *Facing the Future Together:
Report of the United Nations
Secretary-General's Task Force on
Women, Girls and HIV/AIDS in
Southern Africa*, New York: United
Nations.

Vail, L. (1993) *The Creation of Tribal-
ism in Southern Africa*, London:
James Currey.

Van de Walle, N. (2001) *African Econ-
omies and the Politics of Permanent
Crisis, 1979–1999*, Cambridge:
Cambridge University Press.

Waeterloos, E. (2004) 'Land reform in
Zimbabwe: challenges and opportunities for poverty reduction among
commercial farm workers', *World
Development*, XXII(3): 537–553.

Walker, L., G. Reid and M. Cornell
(2004) *Waiting to Happen: HIV/
AIDS in South Africa: The bigger
picture*, London: Lynne Rienner.

Wallensteen, P. and M. Sollenberg

(2001) 'Armed conflict 1989–2000',
Journal of Peace Research,
XXXVIII(5): 629–44.

Wallerstein, I. (1961) *Africa: The
Politics of Independence*, New
York: Vintage Press.

Wanyeki, L. (2003) *Women and Land
in Africa: Culture, Religion and
Realizing Women's Rights*, London:
Zed Books.

Waylen, G. (2006) 'Constitutional
engineering: what opportunities for
the enhancement of gender rights?',
Third World Quarterly, XXVII(7):
1209–21.

Weiss, H., M. Quigley and R. Hayes
(2000) 'Male circumcision and risk
of HIV infection in sub-Saharan
Africa: a systematic review and
meta-analysis', *AIDS*, XIV(15):
2361–70.

Wiggins, S. (2009) 'Are large-scale
commercial farms the answer to
Africa's agricultural prayers?',
Response to Paul Collier, Brighton:
Futures Agriculture Consortium.

Wilkinson, P. (2008) 'Peak oil: threat,
opportunity or phantom?', *Public
Health*, CXXII(7): 664–6.

Woodhouse, P. (2003) 'African
enclosures: A default mode of
development?', *World Development*,
XXXI(10): 1705–20.

— (2009) 'Technology, environment
and the productivity problem in
African agriculture: comment on
the *World Development Report
2008*', *Journal of Agrarian Change*,
IX(2): 263–76.

Wordofa, D. (2004) 'Poverty-reduction
policy responses to gender and
social diversity in Uganda', *Gender
and Development*, XII(1): 68–74.

World Bank (1989) *Women in
Development: Issues for economic
and sector analysis*, Policy Planning
and Research Working Paper

no. 269, Washington, DC: World Bank.

— (1993) *Paradigm Postponed: Gender and Economic Adjustment in Sub-Saharan Africa*, Technical note, Washington, DC: Human Resources and Poverty Division, World Bank.

— (2002) 'Why community-driven development?', in *Poverty Reduction Strategy Sourcebook*, Washington, DC: World Bank.

— (2005) *Agricultural Growth for the Poor. An Agenda for Development*, Washington, DC: World Bank.

— (2007) *World Development Report 2008: Agriculture for development*, Washington, DC: International Bank for Reconstruction and Development/World Bank.

— (2008) *World Development Indicators 2003*, Washington, DC: World Bank.

— (2009) *World Development Report 2009*, Washington, DC: World Bank.

— (2010) *World Development Indicators*, Washington, DC: World Bank.

World Health Organization (WHO) (2008) *The World Health Report 2008: Primary health care now more than ever*, Geneva: World Health Organization.

Yngstrom, I. (2002) 'Women, wives and land rights in Africa: situating gender beyond the household in the debate over land policy and changing tenure systems', *Oxford Development Studies*, XXX(1): 21–40.

Young, K., C. Walkowitz and R. McCallogh (eds) (1981) *Of Marriage and the Market*, Berkeley: University of California Press.

Zartman, I. W. (1964) *The Nigerian Political Scene*, ed. R. O. Tilman and T. Cole, Durham, NC: Duke University Press.

— (1997) 'The international politics of democracy in North Africa', in J. P. Entelis (ed.), *Islam, Democracy and the State in North Africa*, Indianapolis: Indiana University Press.

— (2005) *Cowardly Lions: Missed Opportunities to Prevent State Collapse and Deadly Conflict*, Boulder, CO: Lynne Rienner.

Zimmerman, F. (2000) 'Barriers to participation of the poor in South Africa's land redistribution', *World Development*, XXVIII(8): 1439–60.

Index

About Zed Books

Zed Books is a critical and dynamic publisher, committed to increasing awareness of important international issues and to promoting diversity, alternative voices and progressive social change. We publish on politics, development, gender, the environment and economics for a global audience of students, academics, activists and general readers. Run as a co-operative, Zed Books aims to operate in an ethical and environmentally sustainable way.

Find out more at:

www.zedbooks.co.uk

For up-to-date news, articles, reviews and events information visit:

http://zed-books.blogspot.com

To subscribe to the monthly Zed Books e-newsletter, send an email headed 'subscribe' to:

marketing@zedbooks.net

We can also be found on **Facebook**, **ZNet**, **Twitter** and **Library Thing**.